P9-CDD-647

OPPOSING
VIEWPOINTS®
SERIES

America's Youth

DATE DUE

APR 15 '08	

Other Books of Related Interest:

Opposing Viewpoints Series
Family

Juvenile Crime

Students' Rights

Teen Drug Abuse

Teen Sexuality

Current Controversies Series
School Violence

Teenage Pregnancy and Parenting

Teens and Alcohol

At Issue Series
Child Athletes

Do Children Have Rights?

Should the Voting Age Be Lowered?

Teen Sex

"Congress shall make
no law ... abridging
the freedom of speech,
or of the press."

First Amendment to the U.S. Constitution

The basic foundation of our democracy is the First Amendment guarantee of freedom of expression. The Opposing Viewpoints Series is dedicated to the concept of this basic freedom and the idea that it is more important to practice it than to enshrine it.

OPPOSING VIEWPOINTS® SERIES

America's Youth

Jamuna Carroll, Book Editor

GREENHAVEN PRESS
An imprint of Thomson Gale, a part of The Thomson Corporation

THOMSON

™

GALE

Detroit • New York • San Francisco • New Haven, Conn. • Waterville, Maine • London

THOMSON

GALE

™

Christine Nasso, *Publisher*
Elizabeth Des Chenes, *Managing Editor*

© 2008 The Gale Group.

Star logo is a trademark and Gale and Greenhaven Press are registered trademarks used herein under license.

For more information, contact:
Greenhaven Press
27500 Drake Rd.
Farmington Hills, MI 48331-3535
Or you can visit our Internet site at http://www.gale.com

ISBN-13: 978-0-7377-3735-6 (hardcover)
ISBN-10: 0-7377-3735-2 (hardcover)
ISBN-13: 978-0-7377-3736-3 (pbk.)
ISBN-10: 0-7377-3736-0 (pbk.)

Library of Congress Control Number: 2007935753

Contents

Chapter 3: What Risks Do Youths Face?

Chapter 4: What Would Ensure the Safety and Health of Young Adults?

Why Consider Opposing Viewpoints?

"The only way in which a human being can make some approach to knowing the whole of a subject is by hearing what can be said about it by persons of every variety of opinion and studying all modes in which it can be looked at by every character of mind. No wise man ever acquired his wisdom in any mode but this."

John Stuart Mill

In our media-intensive culture it is not difficult to find differing opinions. Thousands of newspapers and magazines and dozens of radio and television talk shows resound with differing points of view. The difficulty lies in deciding which opinion to agree with and which "experts" seem the most credible. The more inundated we become with differing opinions and claims, the more essential it is to hone critical reading and thinking skills to evaluate these ideas. Opposing Viewpoints books address this problem directly by presenting stimulating debates that can be used to enhance and teach these skills. The varied opinions contained in each book examine many different aspects of a single issue. While examining these conveniently edited opposing views, readers can develop critical thinking skills such as the ability to compare and contrast authors' credibility, facts, argumentation styles, use of persuasive techniques, and other stylistic tools. In short, the Opposing Viewpoints series is an ideal way to attain the higher-level thinking and reading skills so essential in a culture of diverse and contradictory opinions.

In addition to providing a tool for critical thinking, Opposing Viewpoints books challenge readers to question their own strongly held opinions and assumptions. Most people form their opinions on the basis of upbringing, peer pressure, and personal, cultural, or professional bias. By reading carefully balanced opposing views, readers must directly confront new ideas as well as the opinions of those with whom they disagree. This is not to simplistically argue that everyone who reads opposing views will—or should—change his or her opinion. Instead, the series enhances readers' understanding of their own views by encouraging confrontation with opposing ideas. Careful examination of others' views can lead to the readers' understanding of the logical inconsistencies in their own opinions, perspective on why they hold an opinion, and the consideration of the possibility that their opinion requires further evaluation.

Evaluating Other Opinions

To ensure that this type of examination occurs, Opposing Viewpoints books present all types of opinions. Prominent spokespeople on different sides of each issue as well as well-known professionals from many disciplines challenge the reader. An additional goal of the series is to provide a forum for other, less known, or even unpopular viewpoints. The opinion of an ordinary person who has had to make the decision to cut off life support from a terminally ill relative, for example, may be just as valuable and provide just as much insight as a medical ethicist's professional opinion. The editors have two additional purposes in including these less known views. One, the editors encourage readers to respect others' opinions—even when not enhanced by professional credibility. It is only by reading or listening to and objectively evaluating others' ideas that one can determine whether they are worthy of consideration. Two, the inclusion of such viewpoints encourages the important critical thinking skill of objectively evaluating an author's credentials and bias. This evaluation will illuminate an author's reasons for taking a particular stance on an issue and will aid in readers' evaluation of the author's ideas.

It is our hope that these books will give readers a deeper understanding of the issues debated and an appreciation of the complexity of even seemingly simple issues when good and honest people disagree. This awareness is particularly important in a democratic society such as ours in which people enter into public debate to determine the common good. Those with whom one disagrees should not be regarded as enemies but rather as people whose views deserve careful examination and may shed light on one's own.

Thomas Jefferson once said that "difference of opinion leads to inquiry, and inquiry to truth." Jefferson, a broadly educated man, argued that "if a nation expects to be ignorant and free . . . it expects what never was and never will be." As individuals and as a nation, it is imperative that we consider the opinions of others and examine them with skill and discernment. The Opposing Viewpoints series is intended to help readers achieve this goal.

David L. Bender and Bruno Leone,
Founders

Introduction

"Watching shows with sexual content may influence teen sexual behavior, but . . . some viewing effects can be positive."

      —RAND Research Brief

In 2004 the RAND Corporation summarized the findings of two of its studies into the effects of television on young people's sexual attitudes and behaviors. The TV shows teens typically watch, in RAND's contention, contain "heavy doses of sexual content, ranging from touching, kissing, jokes, and innuendo to conversations about sexual activity and portrayal of intercourse." In fact, two of three TV programs include sexual content, and four of five have at least two scenes in which sexual activity is discussed or depicted, according to the Kaiser Family Foundation. Not surprisingly, families and child welfare experts are curious about the effect televised sexuality has on children. Many wonder if exposure to sexual content from a young age may encourage individuals to have sex before they are ready. RAND found that television's portrayal of sex and sexuality has both positive and negative effects on youngsters in the United States.

The idea that sexual content on TV can benefit youths contradicts popular convention. Yet the RAND study reflects an emerging view that such programming has brought teen sexuality to the forefront, where topics that were previously considered taboo can be tackled. Since Americans address sex less freely than people in some other societies, such as those in which public nudity and prostitution are legal, TV may be a major disseminator of information about sex. Ron Whittaker, a professor of broadcasting, emphasizes that the majority of young people receive their knowledge about sex not from their parents, school, or church, but from their peers and the media. Because television is the country's most influential medium, some say it can be used to convey specific information that may help adolescents and teens make healthier choices.

To examine this idea, the Kaiser Family Foundation investigated the impact a single episode of *Friends*, the most popular sitcom in 2003, had on youths. Two main characters on the show had sex and a pregnancy resulted even though they used a condom. In the episode, which attracted an estimated 1.67 million viewers between 12 and 17 years old, the characters discussed specific data regarding the effectiveness of condoms. The majority of young viewers (67 percent) surveyed after the episode recalled the data correctly, and 10 percent of respondents said they talked with an adult about condoms' efficacy because of what they had seen on *Friends*. Television, in some people's opinion, can prompt young viewers to ask questions about safe sex or examine whether they're even ready for sex at all.

Furthermore, some commentators assert that popular shows featuring young characters who are gay, pregnant, abstinent, or infected with STDs can be a launching-off point for family discussions about sex. Elizabeth Schroeder in her article "Using TV as an Ally in Sexuality Education" encourages parents to watch television with their child and analyze it together. Parents can initiate discussion about any action or scene that conveys an important message, whether positive or negative. Some questions she suggests are "What would you do if you were in so-and-so's place?" "What do you think this story says about [kids, women, people of color, the elderly, gay people]?" In this view, seizing on TV's "teachable moments" is a way for parents and their kids to share their values with one another.

Some parents and youth experts claim, however, that the ubiquity of sex on TV ingrains in young people the idea that sex at an early age is normal and acceptable. What's more, they maintain, the way TV programs most often present sex is unrealistic and glamorized. Many characters in soap operas, music videos, primetime shows, and commercials launch into sex without thought or have unprotected sex regularly, which critics believe sets a poor example for children. The RAND researchers discovered that virgin youths who were most exposed to sexual content on TV were twice as likely as those who viewed the least such content to initiate sex during the following year or to advance farther in their sexual activity, such as progressing to heavy kissing or oral sex. According to the findings, even watching shows in which characters discussed sex without engaging in it influenced youngsters. Helen Fields sums up the RAND study in *U.S. News & World Report*:

> Watching TV helps adolescents develop their beliefs about sex, the authors say—so whether it's 'Sex and the City's' Samantha getting it on with a fireman on the back of the truck or just the people on 'Friends' joking about sex, the perception that 'everybody's doing it' seems to get into those adolescent brains.

Those commentators who oppose sexual content in TV programming further counter the claim that TV can be used as a tool to educate youths. They argue that characters rarely discuss STDs, pregnancy, and the emotional consequences of sex, citing statistics from the Kaiser Family Foundation studies that only 3 percent of sex scenes and 15 percent of shows with sexual content mention safe sex or abstinence. Moreover, they note, 15 percent of scenes depicting sexual intercourse involve characters who have just met. Such carefree attitudes about sex, some say, create fodder for such shocking real-life stories as the 2006 report of an eleven-year-old British girl who became pregnant from a one-night stand.

Like television, many other facets of pop culture have an effect on the mindset and behavior of growing children. Whether this influence is a positive or negative force, though, remains disputed. *Opposing Viewpoints: America's Youth* delves into this and other debates revolving around America's youngsters, addressing these questions: What Values Do American Youths Hold? What Behaviors Do Young People Engage In? What Risks Do Youths Face? What Would Ensure the Safety and Health of Young Adults? As evidenced by the diverse views posed by the authors, there is no consensus when it comes to the issue of how best to raise youths to become healthy, moral adults.

**OPPOSING VIEWPOINTS® SERIES**

CHAPTER 1

What Values Do American Youth Hold?

Chapter Preface

A survey by the Harrison Group found that the number of young people who listed materialism as their most important value increased twelve points from 2003 to 2006. Similarly, a Pew Research Center poll conducted in 2006 discovered that 80 percent of people aged 18 to 25 view getting rich as a top life goal of their generation. These statistics alarm youth advocates who believe that values are the ruler by which people measure the appropriateness of their actions and that materialism as a value fails to measure up. Values help shape the lives and beliefs of the country's children and are the basis on which youths make decisions that affect their own and the country's future. The U.S. Department of Education further explains the significance of young people's values: "Those who grow up with strong, consistent and positive values are happier, do better in school and are more likely to contribute to society."

Some youth advocates and parents believe that materialism (valuing "things" like money and possessions) can be unhealthy for young people. They are critical of the idea that material things make youths—or anyone—truly happy. "Compared to their grandparents, today's young adults have grown up with much more affluence, slightly less happiness and much greater risk of depression and assorted social pathology," argues David G. Myers in *American Psychologist*. Indeed, studies link people with a high value on material things to lower life satisfaction. This may be because materialism is difficult to sustain unless one has plenty of money, and also because, according to research, materialistic people have unrealistically high expectations of the happiness and life changes they think material things will bring. One 24-year-old who says he got caught up in wanting "more and more and more" admits, "Yes, I have a nice apartment, a great job, a great degree, great clothing. But I feel empty inside rather often." Conversely, studies show people who are the least materialistic are the most satisfied with their lives.

Other commentators insist that materialism has its place in society. "Materialism is often one of the primary components of the American dream and provides us with a sense of security and the anticipation of happiness," according to an editorial by researchers Suzanne Martin and Emily Zwanziger. In this view, material values fuel progress. In "A (Mild) Defense of Luxury," published in the *Chronicle of Higher Education*, James B. Twitchell supports this idea: "Our love of things is the cause of the Industrial Revolution, not the consequence." For young people, materialism may also be essential for self-expression. The article "What Do the Holidays Mean to Today's Youth?" maintains that "young people define themselves through their choices—the clothes they wear, the music they listen to, the television they watch. . . . They are striving to create their own identities, often using their material possessions as an avenue for self-expression." What's more, some commentators add, the desire for material goods can be appropriately balanced against desires to spend time with family, to hang out with friends, and to be generous. Around holiday time, for example, when consumerism and materialism seem to peak, adolescents and teenagers wish to receive gifts and money while they also value family, friends, religious community, and charity.

"Material things are neither bad nor good," James E. Burroughs comments. "It is the role and status they are accorded in one's life that can be problematic." Judging by the discussions many Americans are having, they, like the authors in the next chapter, are concerned with identifying and evaluating the values teenagers in the United States hold as well as exploring their implications for the future.

*"Young voters turned out, and they did
so as never before."*

Teenagers Value Their Vote

David C. King

*David C. King argues in the following viewpoint that more
young Americans voted in 2004 than in any election since 1972.
What's more, he asserts, the exit polls did not count the nearly
three million college students and other young people who
planned to vote by absentee ballot. He attributes the high turnout to both Republicans' and Democrats' get-out-the-vote efforts
that year. In King's opinion, young people are changing the face
of politics by basing their vote on their own religious or moral
beliefs rather than strict party dogma. King is associate director
of the School of Government at Harvard University.*

As you read, consider the following questions:

1. According to author David C. King, how many more
   young Americans voted in 2004 than in 2000?
2. According to the author, which youths should both parties court?
3. In the author's view, young voters supported John Kerry
   as a reaction against what?

David C. King, "Youth Came Through with Big Turnout," *Boston Globe*, November 4,
2004. Reproduced by permission of the author.

America's young people were buzzing about the presidential campaign before Election Day [2004]. College towns saw sky-high registration numbers, and young adults told pollsters they planned to vote. What happened?

Despite long lines and registration snafus, voters under age 30 clocked the highest turnout percentage since 1972. The good news is that America's young people are more engaged in politics than at any time in two generations. Aging cynics have been quick to blame the kids for a host of political lapses, but the cynics have it wrong.

More Young Voters

Start with the numbers. According to Professor William Galston at the University of Maryland, at least 20.9 million Americans under 30 voted on Tuesday. That is an increase of 4.6 million voters from 2000. Four years ago, just 42.3 percent of young people voted. This year more than 51.6 percent did.

Young people were especially active in battleground states, with turnout at 64.4 percent of eligible voters. Furthermore, these estimates understate things, because college kids are more likely than other groups (except the military) to vote by absentee ballot. Surveys of college students around the country, done in the weeks before the election, found 42 percent of students planning to vote absentee. Exit polls completely miss these young voters who numbered, this year, close to 3 million.

According to exit polls, Senator John Kerry won the under-30 set with 54 percent of the vote to President [George W.] Bush's 44 percent. The Democrats lost every other age group. Without young Democrat voters, President Bush would have rolled to victory in Wisconsin and New Hampshire; Iowa and Nevada, too, would have been much bigger wins for the president. In political circles today, Democrats are blaming young Americans for not showing up, and Republicans are

Kids Voting USA Involves Youths in the Election Process

Kids Voting USA is a program in which children participate in a mock vote and accompany their parents to the polls on Election Day. Reports show that even this modest gesture to including youth increased the interest in voting of their whole family. Parents were more likely to discuss politics with their kids and thus an estimated 600,000 adult voters were more likely to vote because of it. . . .

Including youth in a real, substantive way in politics will lead to even more interest as they take their public-spirited nature into the political realm.

National Youth Rights Association,
"Top Ten Reasons to Lower the Voting Age." www.youthrights.org.

chortling over their allegedly low turnout. Nonsense. Rather, both parties should be seeing their future in the eyes of young voters.

Turnout was up among every demographic group this year, thanks to an impressive get-out-the-vote effort by both parties. Young people were the ground troops that visited voters door-to-door and manned phone banks for both parties on Election Day.

A New Political Worldview

Democrats should not take much comfort, though, in the partisanship of the young Americans. According to research by Harvard's Institute of Politics and pollster John Della Volpe, most college students no longer fit neatly along a liberal to conservative continuum. Their support for John Kerry was largely a reaction against President Bush's actions in Iraq [when, in 2003, he authorized an invasion of Iraq, which drew controversy], while they judged President Bush to be a stronger leader with a more "authentic" personal style.

Earlier this year, we [Harvard University's School of Government] asked a national random sample of college students their opinions on a range of issues. Using a statistical technique called "cluster analysis," we looked at how answers to one question predicted answers to others. What emerged was clear evidence of two political worldviews among young people. The first worldview, which accounts for 49 percent of college students, fits the old definitions of liberals and conservatives. The second worldview, amounting to 51 percent of students, is neither liberal nor conservative. These young voters base political judgments on religious and moral grounds. They fall into two distinct camps: religious centrists and secular centrists, and neither group is predictably conservative or liberal. Young religious centrists, for example, tend to support universal healthcare and affirmative action, while simultaneously calling for an end to gay marriage. Religious centrists are more likely than their secular counterparts to vote, and both parties will need to court them. There is a new religiosity among America's young people. Their burst of activism in both parties comes from deep convictions about caring for the poor, for their communities, and for families. Community volunteerism is at an all-time high. So is church attendance. While 29 percent of the general public call themselves "born again Christians," fully 35 percent of college students embrace the label. The new battleground of American politics—with young voters as the ground troops—will be over how to address the moral idealism of today's youth. Will it be a version of community found in Jesus' *Sermon on the Mount,* or will it be more akin to the Book of Revelations? Among the religious centrists—those crucial swing voters for both parties—the very definitions of "politics" and "community" are at stake.

So, yes, the young voters turned out, and they did so as never before. That news alone may frighten the political establishment. Old line partisans of the left and right can no longer ignore these young voters.

> "The youth vote is bunk. It's a mirage.
> Fool's gold."

Teenagers Do Not Value Their Vote

Jonah Goldberg

Jonah Goldberg is editor-at-large of National Review Online, *which offers conservative views on politics and news. In the viewpoint that follows, Goldberg charges that efforts to motivate young Americans to vote in 2004 failed just as miserably as they have during every election since 1972. He blames Democrats and the media for hyping the value of the youth vote. Young people's interest in politics, Goldberg argues, has declined ever since the draft was eliminated and is now shallow at best. Therefore, he concludes, it is unreasonable to expect youths to help enact any real political change in the United States.*

As you read, consider the following questions:

1. According to Goldberg, what was the argument for lowering the voting age in the United States?
2. In the author's view, how did youth politics change once the draft was eliminated?

3. How does Goldberg respond to statistics that more young Americans voted in 2004 than in 2000?

"This is the best election night in history," Democratic National Committee [DNC] Chair Terry McAuliffe declared at 8 P.M. on Tuesday [November 2, 2004]. Rumors around Washington suggest that he changed his position shortly thereafter.

Now, I might be expected to have thought—as someone who was pulling for [President George W.] Bush (or, to be more accurate, pulling against [Senator John] Kerry)—that Tuesday evening ended up being the best election night in history. And that's about right, except for the sad news that as much as half of America's youth is about to die. Or Lord knows what percentage of black voters.

You see, I get confused, because it was never entirely clear to me whether [rapper] Sean "P. Diddy" Combs's "Vote or Die" racket [his campaign to encourage voting] was aimed at blacks or at young people—at black young people, or at white young people who like to dress like black young people. Or was it simply a way for him to move merchandise and get more publicity from MTV? In any case, this year's turnout among young people and blacks was, as a proportion of the whole electorate, almost identical to 2000's.

The repercussions of the DNC's failure to scare or otherwise motivate blacks into voting in huge numbers can be dealt with another time. That's a serious enough issue that it doesn't deserve the sort of mockery and scorn I'm about to heap on the "youth vote."

The Myth of the Youth Vote

The youth vote is bunk. It's a mirage. Fool's gold. A Nietzschean vital lie. A will-o'-the-wisp. A media confabulation. Nonsense. Hooey. Baloney, bilge, hogwash, and hooey.

But let me put aside the Kerrian nuance for a moment and tell you what I really think.

The notion that young people are some vast, untapped pool of liberal or—even better!—leftist voters has never, ever, been proven true. For years, '60s-radical types, liberals, and universal-suffrage fetishists insisted that the voting age should be dropped from 21 to 18. "Their non-partisan" argument was a legitimate one: If you can be drafted to fight and die for your country, you should be able to vote.

The more sincere hope on the left was that these masses of idealistic, newly enfranchised youngsters would sweep liberal politicians into office and horrible, mean fogies like [President] Richard Nixon out. This was perfectly consistent with the cult of youth that began with the French Revolution and extended through the first true modern youth movements of the 20th century: Italian and German fascism.

Anyway, when the United States dropped the voting age to 18 in 1972, young people did vote in record numbers, but not along strikingly partisan lines: 52 percent went for [Senator] George McGovern and 48 percent for Richard Nixon. Nixon won reelection handily, of course, and McGovern went on to become synonymous with everything that was wrong with the Democratic party in the 1970s (and, to some extent, even today). Meanwhile, after 1972, turnout by young voters decreased steadily for decades.

The main reason youth politics fizzled is that once the draft was eliminated, young people stopped being politicized and started being commercialized. The '60s "youth movement" became simply a self-indulgent consumer culture centered around sex, drugs, and rock and roll. But in their pampered and self-absorbed way, baby boomers continued to insist they were a vitally important political force, that being authentically young was being authentically political. And they've never gotten over that conceit.

The Hallmark of Apathetic Youth

I ... know what you're thinking. The hallmark of the apathetic youth: Politics don't interest you because they don't apply to you. Legislators don't care about you. Politicians can't relate to you, and you can't relate to politicians. Whoever the president is, he really has no effect on you whatsoever.

Quite frankly, that argument is crap. It's a lazy cop-out of an excuse. I know. I've used it.

Kristin Brown. "Exercising Our Freedom,"
Cavalier Daily, January 30, 2004.

No Youth Movement

Today [in 2004], the self-proclaimed "youth movement" is simply a youth auxiliary of the Democratic party. Baby-boomer liberals still fall for the rhetoric of the young, partly because they fervently hope to exploit this huge, untapped reservoir of votes, and partly because nostalgia for their own radical salad days has corrupted their political analysis.

Most young people do not take any great pride in being young. Why should they? Being young requires no work and no investment in mental or physical resources. It says almost nothing about a person's real beliefs. Youth politics is as deep as the paint on a can of Diet Pepsi and has about as much substance on the inside.

It's true that this year young voters turned out in higher numbers than in 2000, but they made up exactly the same proportion of the overall electorate: 17 percent. And while Kerry may have done better among young voters than Bush did, the numbers were spectacularly underwhelming. Only Pennsylvania saw a proportional surge in youth voting.

Remember how we were all told that the new army of young "Deaniacs" was going to carry [2004 presidential nominee] Howard Dean to the White House because of the unprecedented enthusiasm, idealism, and youthful vigah (as [President] John Kennedy would say)? Well, that fizzled like a North Korean light bulb. The same was true for John Kerry.

And when the youth didn't show up, countless pundits echoed the words of pro-Kerry journalist Andrew Sullivan: "We were all suckered."

No we "all" weren't. Only those who wanted to be were. And they fall for it every time.

> "For four out of five college students,
> religion's importance does not diminish
> at all. Faith simply remains in the
> background."

College Students Value Religion

Mark D. Regnerus and Jeremy E. Uecker

According to Mark D. Regnerus and Jeremy E. Uecker in the following viewpoint, college does not destroy students' faith, as many Americans believe, and can in fact foster religious growth. Although fewer young people attend church during their college years, they do retain their religiosity, the authors claim. Students' faith merely becomes more private during this time, Regnerus and Uecker contend. Furthermore, they maintain, surveys reveal that college students consider their religion more important to them than do people their age who do not attend college. Regnerus is an assistant professor of sociology and Uecker is a graduate student at The University of Texas at Austin.

As you read, consider the following questions:

1. According to Regnerus and Uecker, what is it about college that supposedly places young adults at odds with their religion?

Mark D. Regnerus and Jeremy E. Uecker, "How Corrosive Is College to Religious Faith and Practice?" Social Science Research Council, February 5, 2007. Reproduced by permission.

2. What are three reasons that religion is not expected to influence or be influenced by college education, in the authors' contention?

3. In the authors' opinion, what example reinforces the notion that few students drop their faith due to their professors' teachings?

While Americans remain among the most religious in the industrialized world, it is widely observed that many of them exhibit cycles of religiosity, the most evident of which occurs in early adulthood. The young adult years of many Americans are marked by a clear decline in outward religious expression, which is widely thought to hit bottom during—and perhaps because of—the college experience. Data from 30 years of the General Social Survey pinpoints age 22 as the point in the life course when average levels of weekly or more frequent church attendance are at their lowest (17 percent). The climb back into regular or semi-regular religious practice—if it occurs at all, and it usually does—is often stimulated by marriage and childbearing. This barely needs retelling, as if a farewell to organized religion during the college years is simply part of the cultural script so many possess. But not *all* Americans check their religion at the dorm door. While much is made of religious decline, emerging adulthood is also a time in the life course when Americans are most open to religious change and growth. It is a phase commonly associated with religious conversion and thus targeted for considerable proselytizing by evangelical religious organizations. Waxing or waning, adolescence and early adulthood are certainly the most religiously unstable phases of the life course.

Waning religiosity is typically the presumed phenomenon, however, and various reasons have been offered for why very many young Americans tend to experience a dip in religiousness during the college years. The common suspects are the secularizing tendencies of higher education and the cognitive dissonance (or guilt) caused by deviation from (religious) norms taught by parents. First, it has been popularly held that the university classroom expands students' horizons, breaks down the "believability" of religious faith, and for such reasons constitutes "a breeding ground for apostasy" [as explained by authors David Caplovitz and Fred Sherrow]. Additionally, many believe greater personal freedom affords emerging adults the opportunity to stop activities (like going to church) that they find uninteresting or devalued among peers, and to start doing things they are curious about and motivated (by peers) to do—things like drinking, drug use, and sex—that place them at odds with their religious tradition's teachings. As a result, higher education and its freedoms are thought to promote more secularized perspectives on the world—or at least ones at odds with a particular religious socialization, which in turn may lead some young adults to stop believing in the religion of their youth. . . .

College Students Are More Religious than Other Young Adults

So what can be said about the religiosity of today's young adults? As we might expect, recent data from the Add Health [National Longitudinal Study of Adolescent Health] study reveals that nearly 70 percent of all young adults who attended church at least once a month during high school subsequently curtailed their church attendance. Contrary to our own and others' expectations, however, young adults who *never enrolled* in college are presently the *least* religious young Americans. The assumption that the religious involvement of young people diminishes when they attend college is of course true: 64 percent of those currently enrolled in a traditional four-year institution have curbed their attendance habits. Yet, 76 percent of those who *never enrolled* in college report a decline in religious service attendance.

Attendance habits are the hardest hit during early adult-hood. But some forms of religiosity, like how important religion is in one's life, witness far smaller declines. More than one in four young adults who avoid college reported lower "religious salience" than when interviewed as adolescents, compared with just 19 percent of young adults pursuing a traditional college education. And then there is religious disaffiliation—when youth no longer identify with any religious affiliation at all. Whereas 20 percent of those that did not pursue college renounced any and all religious affiliation, only 13 percent of four-year college students had done the same.

Some, Not All, Youths Are at Risk

Thus, the assumption that a college education is the *reason* for such a decline gathers little support. The results remain the same even when we employ multiple regression models to account for other factors that might explain the college-religion relationship (such as age, marriage, drinking habits, and sexual behavior, to name a few). Simply put: Higher education is *not* the enemy of religiosity. Instead, young people who avoid college altogether display a more precipitous drop in their religious participation. So if a college education is not the secularizing force we often presume it to be, what is going on?. . .

Why don't we see evidence of education-inspired secularization? Anecdotally, such a phenomenon is well-known to many academic professionals. They have *seen* students stop believing. We would argue, however, that this too is often the result not of education, but again of processes set in motion long before young people ever set foot on a college campus: Those students who "lose their faith" in college or drop out of organized religion after high school are primarily those already at considerable risk of doing so *for other reasons* that predate these actions. To suggest the die is cast before the dorm room is occupied may be too strong a claim, but not by much. As Christian Smith and Melinda Denton (2005) note in

Religion Remains Important to College Students

Students today come to college with a solid core of beliefs about politics, political involvement, community service and religion. A wide majority of college students (70%) says that religion plays an important rote in their lives. One in four (25%) report that they have become more spiritual since entering college while just seven percent (7%) say they have become less spiritual. In terms of the religious make-up on college campuses, twenty-five percent (25%) of students are Protestant, twenty-four percent (24%) are Catholic, eighteen percent (18%) are Fundamentalist/Evangelical Christian, three percent (3%) are Jewish, one percent (1%) are Muslim, thirteen percent (13%) are some other religion and sixteen percent (16%) have no religious preference.

Harvard University Institute of Politics,
Redefining Political Attitudes and Activism, *April 11, 2006.*

Soul Searching, parents tend to "get what they are" when it comes to their teenagers' religious sense. If parents do not actively affirm and transmit the oral and written traditions of a religion, their failure to "teach the language" results in youth who cannot speak the language and are at elevated risk of shedding the religious value system altogether. Indeed, scholars often forget that religion is primarily taught, not caught or transmitted by osmosis. Once these teenagers leave the structures (especially families) that have patterned their religious lives, religiosity is simply left behind as well.

Religious Beliefs Are Rarely Challenged at Universities

The majority of college students, however, do not exhibit a noticeable decline in the importance of faith in their lives.

The religious belief systems of most students go largely un-
touched for the duration of their education. Religious faith
lies dormant in students' lives, waiting to be awakened at
some point after college, but it is rarely seen as something
that could either influence or be influenced by the educational
process. This is true for several reasons. First, some students
have elected not to engage in the intellectual life around them.
They are there to pursue an "applicable" degree, among other,
more mundane pursuits. This is hardly limited to religious
university students, though. Second, some "miss the forest for
the trees," wishing instead to stick to what will be on the
exam. Here again, there is nothing uniquely religious about
this pathway. Such students are numerous, and as a result
students' own religious faith (or lack of it) faces little challenge. Indeed, many university curricula are constructed to re-
ward this type of intellectual disengagement. The modern
university seems increasingly interested in certifying students,
boosting their technical skill set, and offering, as one example,
money-generating "crash course" Weekend curriculums, all of
which are quite distinct from previous emphases on the liberal arts and communication skills. One byproduct of this is
that grappling with the deeper realities of religion, faith, the
nature of knowledge, and human meaning seldom occurs.
Courses on computer programming or electrical engineering
are religiously neutral. What is not contested, then, cannot be
lost. Third, while higher education opens up new worlds for
students who apply themselves, it can but doesn't often create
skepticism about old (religious) worlds, or at least not among
most American young people, in part because there is not a
great deal of *perceived competition* between higher education
and faith, and because very many young Americans are so
under-socialized in their religious faith (before college begins)
that they would have difficulty recognizing faith-challenging
material when it appears. And even if they did perceive a challenge, many young people do not consider religion something
worth arguing over.

Private Religiosity

As a result, while their church attendance may take a hit simply because of the late-night orientation of college life, or because of collective norms about appearing "too religious," very many young people nevertheless retain a static level of private religiosity during their college years. Recall that for four out of five college students, religion's importance does not diminish at all. Faith simply remains in the background of students' lives as a part of who they are, but not a part they talk about much with their peers or professors (and for many, this never changes across the life course). In structured class debates about some of the "big questions" of life—such as the sources of happiness, the nature of love, and the meaning of sex—we have witnessed such "closet Christians" become animated (albeit briefly) seemingly out of nowhere when we began to talk about elemental ideas close to the heart of religion. Such experiences reinforce the data that the number of college students who altogether drop religious faith due to cognitive inconsistencies that their professors point out is very small. Far more commonly, faith goes underground not for the purpose of feeding and sustaining it through the college years but simply because it feels non-normative to either admit religious faith, much less make any sort of big deal about it. As Smith and Denton (2005) note in their study of teenagers, so with young adults: to appear over-religious can be the social kiss of death.

On the other hand are devoutly religious college students. They arrive on campus *expecting* challenges and hostility to their religious perspectives. When they don't get it, they're pleasantly surprised; when they do, it merely meets their expectations and fits within their expected narrative about college life. Campus religious organizations anticipate such intellectual challenge, and often provide a forum for like-minded students. In fact, college campuses are less hostile to organized religious expression and its retention than are other contexts encountered by emerging adults, such as the workplace. The arrival of postmodern, post-positivist thought on university campuses has served to legitimize religiosity, even in intellectual circles. Together with heightened emphasis on religious tolerance, antireligious hostility on campus may even be at a decades-long low.

"Most [twentysomethings] pull away
from participation and engagement in
Christian churches, particularly during
the 'college years.'"

College Students Lose
Interest in Religion

Barna Group

The Barna Group provides leadership and resources to guide
Americans' spiritual transformation. From 2001 to 2006 it interviewed thousands of teens and adults about their religious activity, and the viewpoint that follows summarizes its findings. The
organization insists that many young people, though strongly
spiritual in their teen years, leave church behind when they
reach their twenties. Of those who used to attend church, 61 percent spend less time reading the Bible, attending church, and
praying than older adults, Barna Group claims. To counter this,
the organization suggests that youth ministries must focus on
fostering faith that sustains beyond high school.

As you read, consider the following questions:

1. In the organization's view, in what six religious activities
   do twentysomethings participate less often than older
   adults?

2. Why does deep, lasting spiritual transformation rarely
occur among teens, according to the Barna Group leader
quoted in the viewpoint?

3. How did the study's authors classify "evangelicals"?

Transitions in life are rarely simple. Some of the most significant and complex shifts that people undergo occur
during the transition from adolescence to early adulthood. An
important part of that maturation is the refinement of people's
spiritual commitment and behavior.

A new study by The Barna Group (Ventura, California)
shows that despite strong levels of spiritual activity during the
teen years, most twentysomethings disengage from active participation in the Christian faith during their young adult
years—and often beyond that. In total, six out of ten twentysomethings were involved in a church during their teen years,
but have failed to translate that into active spirituality during
their early adulthood.

Teens Embrace Spirituality

Teenagers thrive on fresh experiences and new perspectives.
The spiritual dimension gives teens a fertile ground for their
explorations. Half of teens attend a church-related service or
activity in a typical week. More than three-quarters discuss
matters of faith with peers and three out of five teens attend
at least one youth group meeting at a church during a typical
three month period. One-third of teenagers say they participate in a Christian club on campus at some point during a
typical school year. There is also a substantial amount of un-
orthodox spiritual activity: three-quarters of America's teenaged youths have engaged in at least one type of psychic or
witchcraft-related activity during their teen years (not including reading horoscopes).

Still, one of the most striking findings from the research is
the broad base of opportunities that Christian churches in

America have to work with teenagers. Overall, more than four out of five teens say they have attended a church for a period of at least two months during their teenage years (81%). This represents substantial penetration and significant prospects for influencing the nation's 24 million teens.

Disengagement of Older Youths

At the same time, the Barna research underscores how fleeting that influence may be: twentysomethings continue to be the most spiritually independent and resistant age group in America. Most of them pull away from participation and engagement in Christian churches, particularly during the "college years." The research shows that, compared to older adults, twentysomethings have significantly lower levels of church attendance, time spent alone studying and reading the Bible, volunteering to help churches, donations to churches, Sunday school and small group involvement, and use of Christian media (including television, radio and magazines).

In fact, the most potent data regarding disengagement is that a majority of twentysomethings—61% of today's [2006] young adults—had been churched at one point during their teen years but they are now spiritually disengaged (i.e., not actively attending church, reading the Bible, or praying). Only one-fifth of twentysomethings (20%) have maintained a level of spiritual activity consistent with their high school experiences. Another one-fifth of teens (19%) were never significantly reached by a Christian community of faith during their teens and have remained disconnected from the Christian faith.

For most adults, this pattern of disengagement is not merely a temporary phase in which they test the boundaries of independence, but is one that continues deeper into adulthood, with those in their thirties also less likely than older adults to be religiously active. Even the traditional impulse of parenthood—when people's desire to supply spiritual guidance for their children pulls them back to church—is weakening. The new research pointed out that just one-third of twentysomethings who are parents regularly take their children to church, compared with two-fifths of parents in their thirties and half of parents who are 40-years-old or more.

David Kinnaman, the director of the research, pointed out, "There is considerable debate about whether the disengagement of twentysomethings is a lifestage issue—that is, a predictable element in the progression of people's development as they go through various family, occupational and chronological stages—or whether it is unique to this generation. While there is some truth to both explanations, this debate misses the point, which is that the current state of ministry to twentysomethings is woefully inadequate to address the spiritual needs of millions of young adults. These individuals are making significant life choices and determining the patterns and preferences of their spiritual reality while churches wait, generally in vain, for them to return after college or when the kids come. When and if young adults do return to churches, it is difficult to convince them that a passionate pursuit of Christ is anything more than a nice add-on to their cluttered lifestyle."

Piecing Faith Together

While twentysomethings often disengage from traditional religious expressions, faith and spirituality are hardly absent from their lives. The research also examined a number of significant realities about the spiritual journeys of young adults:

- As for religious identity, most twentysomethings maintain outward allegiance to Christianity: 78% of twentysomethings say they are Christians, compared with 83% of teenagers. Although they are less likely than older generations to feel this way, most twentysomethings describe themselves as "deeply spiritual."

- Loyalty to congregations is one of the casualties of young adulthood: twentysomethings were nearly 70% more likely than older adults to strongly assert that if they "cannot find a local church that will help them become more like Christ, then they will find people and groups that will, and connect with them instead of a local church." They are also significantly less likely to believe that "a person's faith in God is meant to be developed by involvement in a local church."

- These attitudes explain other anomalies of twentysomething spirituality. Much of the activity of young adults, such as it is, takes place outside congregations. Young adults were just as likely as older Americans to attend special worship events not sponsored by a local church, to participate in a spiritually oriented small group at work, to have a conversation with someone else who holds them accountable for living faith principles, and to attend a house church not associated with a conventional church. Interestingly, there was one area in which the spiritual activities of twentysomethings outpaced their predecessors: visiting faith-related websites.

- The intensity of religious commitment is lower among young adults, but not as low as might be assumed. Among those in their twenties and thirties, 6% have beliefs that qualify them as evangelical. This is statistically on par with the level among today's teenagers (5%), but about half the rate of those over age 40 (12%). One-third of young adults (36%) qualify as born again Christians, which is slightly lower than the 44% of those over 40. (In the Barna survey, evangelicals and born again Christians are

defined based upon religious beliefs and commit-
ments, not based on the terms people use to describe themselves.)

Where Youth Ministry Is Failing

Kinnaman offered several insights about the data: "Much of
the ministry to teenagers in America needs an overhaul—not
because churches fail to attract significant numbers of young
people, but because so much of those efforts are not creating
a sustainable faith beyond high school. There are certainly effective youth ministries across the country, but the levels of
disengagement among twentysomethings suggest that youth
ministry fails too often at discipleship and faith formation. A
new standard for viable youth ministry should be not the
number of attenders, the sophistication of the events, or the
'cool' factor of the youth group but whether teens have the
commitment, passion and resources to pursue Christ inten-
tionally and whole-heartedly after they leave the youth ministry nest."

The Strategic Leader of The Barna Group explained that,
"It's not entirely surprising that deep, lasting spiritual transformation rarely happens among teenagers—it's hard work at
any age, let alone with the distractions of youth. And, since
teenagers' faith often mirrors the intensity of their parents,
youth workers face steep challenges because they are trying to
impart something of spiritual significance that teenagers generally do not receive from home.

"Our team is conducting more research into what leads to
a sustainable faith, but we have already observed some key en-
hancements that youth workers may consider. One of those is
to be more personalized in ministry. Every teen has different
needs, questions and doubts, so helping them to wrestle
through those specific issues and to understand God's unique
purpose for their lives is significant. The most effective

churches have set up leadership development tracks and mentoring processes to facilitate this type of personalization.

"Another shift," he continued, "is to develop teenagers' ability to think and process the complexities of life from a biblical viewpoint. This is not so much about having the right head knowledge as it is about helping teens respond to situations and decisions in light of God's principles for life. Also, we have learned that effective youth ministries do not operate in isolation but have a significant role in training parents to minister to their own children.

"Above all, remember to keep a balanced perspective," Kinnaman cautioned. "Some have overstated the problem, while others minimize it. The fact is millions of American teenagers and twentysomethings are alive to God and devoted to His Kingdom. But the research is also clear that there are significant issues related to the way young people experience and express their faith. Without objectively and strategically addressing those challenges, Christian leaders will miss the opportunity to awaken many more young souls to a life-long zeal for God."

Research Method

The data in this report are based on interviews with more than 22,103 adults and 2,124 teenagers from across the nation in 25 separate surveys. The adult sample included interviews with 3,583 twentysomethings. The Barna Group conducted these studies through the use of telephone and online surveys, implemented from January 2001 through August 2006. All of these projects are based upon random samples of adults and teenagers living within the 48 continental states. The maximum sampling error for any of the nationwide adult studies (which include a minimum of 1,000 interviews) is ±3.2 percentage points at the 95% confidence level. The maximum sampling error for any of the teenage studies (which have a minimum sample of 600 interviews) is ±4.1 percentage points at the 95% confidence level.

In each survey, the distribution of respondents corresponded to the geographic dispersion of the U.S. population. Multiple callbacks were used to increase the probability of including a reliable distribution of qualified individuals. Statistical weighting was used to calibrate the aggregate sample to known population percentages.

"Born again Christians" are defined as people who said they have made a personal commitment to Jesus Christ that is still important in their life today and who also indicated they believe that when they die they will go to Heaven because they had confessed their sins and had accepted Jesus Christ as their savior. Respondents are *not* asked to describe themselves as "born again."

"Evangelicals" meet the born again criteria (described above) *plus* seven other conditions. Those include saying their faith is very important in their life today; believing they have a personal responsibility to share their religious beliefs about Christ with non-Christians; believing that Satan exists; believing that eternal salvation is possible only through grace, not works; believing that Jesus Christ lived a sinless life on earth; asserting that the Bible is accurate in all that it teaches; and describing God as the all-knowing, all-powerful, perfect deity who created the universe and still rules it today. Being classified as an evangelical is not dependent upon church attendance or the denominational affiliation of the church attended. Respondents were *not* asked to describe themselves as "evangelical."

VIEWPOINT

"Teenage children have developed a love affair with the home computer."

Teens Value Technology

Peggy Kendall

Peggy Kendall, associate professor of communications at Bethel University, studies and writes about young people's cyberspace habits. In the following viewpoint she proclaims that American youngsters are dependent on technology to meet complex social needs in ways that were never possible before. Youths use instant messaging and social networking sites, she contends, to manage social relationships, express their individuality, and even get help with homework. However, Kendall cautions, technology can also cause misunderstandings and serve as an avenue for young people to bully their peers. In any case, teenagers will likely continue to value the technologies that are so significant to them today, she concludes.

As you read, consider the following questions:

1. What does Kendall say to support her statement that young people have developed a love affair with their computer?
2. What might a user profile on a social networking site include, according to the author?

Peggy Kendall, "Help! My Kid's Best Friend Is a Computer," *Bethel Focus*, vol. 57, fall 2006. Reproduced by permission.

3. In Kendall's contention, what are idealized responses
   and what two problems can arise from them?

It's 3:30 P.M. The bus pulls up and Jennifer emerges, back-
pack in hand. In a flash, she zips through the front door,
drops her books on the table, and sits down to spend some
quality time with her best friend—before uttering a word,
she's logged on.

To parents who watch this daily ritual, it can seem their
teenage children have developed a love affair with the home
computer. After all, they spend lots of time together, they depend on their computer to meet complex social needs, and
they seem to feel great anguish when they can't be together.
Without question, the computer has become an important
part of life for many American teenagers. Unfortunately, most
parents aren't sure what to make of that fact.

Today's young people have turned to technology to help
them manage friendships and express themselves in a way that
most adults have never experienced. What used to be done
over the phone, in the mall, at the malt shop, and in the sand-
lot is now accomplished in cyberspace. Let's face it. It isn't
easy being a parent who, on one hand, has to struggle to keep
up with the technology kids use so easily, and on the other
hand, must worry about sexual predators, online stalkers, and
kids getting sucked into a cybervortex where they turn pasty
white and lose the ability to talk with real human beings. So,
what are the options? Unplug the computer? Force kids to
watch multiple episodes of *The Andy Griffith Show*? Or ignore
the computer and just hope the whole thing will go away?

It's Big and It's Here to Stay

Whether we like it or not, today's teenagers routinely use the
computer to manage their social lives. Unlike Pong, Michael
Jackson, and 8-tracks, it's a cultural phenomenon that's not
going away. According to the Pew Internet and American Life

project released in 2005, Instant Messenger is used by almost two-thirds of all American adolescents. In addition, social networking websites such as MySpace.com have quietly become one of the fastest-growing uses of the Internet. [According to a 2006 article in *The New Republic*,] MySpace boasts over 55 million users, adding 85,000 new profiles each day—that's 59 new profiles in the time it will take you to read this article! The bottom line is that while the specific technology might change, the way young people communicate with each other has been fundamentally transformed.

The Basics

One of the most common ways young people communicate with each other via the computer (or their cell phone) is through Instant Messenger (IM). According to America Online (AOL), Instant Messenger is "a free online service that lets you communicate with family, friends, and co-workers in real time. Using a buddy list feature, you can see when your buddies are online and available to instant message."

While IM allows people to engage in private conversations in real time, many teenagers also enjoy the option of hanging out with a group of friends at their own leisure. That's where social networking sites come in. On these sites, users create a profile or self-description that may include everything from music, poetry, and original art to pictures of friends, personality quizzes, and random thoughts about life. Teens then regularly check their friends' sites to see what's new. While MySpace is currently the largest social networking site, there are many others, including Facebook (a favorite of Bethel [University] students), Xanga, Friendster, and even some Christian sites like Christianster.com and Oaktree.com.

The challenge of this technology is that it fundamentally changes the way communication takes place. In an effort to understand better the implications of these changes, a research team that included a number of undergraduate students from

Teens Are Plugged In

Although there is some overlap because of the simultaneous use of more than one media, teens estimate that they are spending a whopping 72 hours per week electronically—with TV, Internet, music, video games, cell phoning and text messaging. This places teens at the center of their own private universe, where they can define themselves on their own terms. This generation is committed to communicating with each other, accepting little outside influence.

Social network sites are booming and are becoming paramount in teen interaction. Fully 68% of teens have created profiles on MySpace, Zanga or Facebook. Interestingly, more than one-quarter of teens keeps in touch daily or nearly every day with friends they met online through IM [Instant Messenger], email, message boards or chat rooms. The average teen IMs with 35 people for three hours a week. In contrast, the same teen will call or email each week with only seven people not on the teen's IM list.

Harrison Group, "Flagship Study of America's Youth Describes What Teens Want," November 2006. www.harrisongroupinc.com.

the Department of Communication Studies at Bethel University conducted interviews, focus groups, and surveys with students, parents, and youth pastors about Instant Messenger and social networking sites.

Some Good Things

The clearest finding was that young people truly enjoy using the computer to connect with friends. Not only is it convenient and fun, but it can be an important way for young people to learn how to develop and deepen relationships. A majority of surveyed IM'ers said they felt closer to those friends they regularly IM'd. They were better able to keep in touch, and even help their friends deal with tough issues so that the face-to-face time they spent together was of a perceived higher quality. IM'ers also felt the technology increased their confidence and ability to articulate themselves in a safe environment. Take, for example, one middle school girl. "I IM a lot of boys from my class," she said. "We've gotten to be pretty good friends, which is weird since, if we talked at school, everyone would think we were in love or something." Other IM'ers appreciate a technology that lets them keep in touch with friends or family members who travel or live far away. A final benefit consistently mentioned by teenage IM'ers was that, in spite of what their parents might think, it really did help them do homework.

Some of the Bad Things

While most IM'ers and parents agree that there are certain benefits associated with online communication technology, there are also significant challenges. One of the biggest problems has to do with a lack of shared meaning. Because important nonverbal cues are left out on the computer, users have to imagine what those cues might be—thus creating their own interpretation of how the other person is responding.

These "idealized responses" can foster a number of problems. First, because IM'ers may not be sharing true understanding with the people they interact with, they may be less able to genuinely empathize with their friends or work out conflicts that require them to see problems from another person's perspective. Second, idealized responses can create an environment of "hyperintimacy." When someone is having a conversation late at night, it is easy to imagine a feeling of closeness. Some IM'ers and personal website users say it's almost like writing in a journal. The problem arises when the disclosures are not appropriate for the relationships. It may artificially speed up romantic relationships or create awkward expectations in emerging friendships. Trust is easily broken when teens share too much with "friends" who are not truly friends.

A third problem has to do with bad behavior. When asked why high schoolers thought it was easier to be mean to someone online than in person, one student offered: "When you are on the computer, you don't have to see the hurt in their eyes." Most young IM'ers reported being the victim of some type of gossip, bullying, deception, or just plain meanness at the hands of another. Some students, especially middle-school boys, felt freer to swear and say things online that they would never say in person. Middle schoolers were also more reluctant to report online bad behavior since it "didn't seem quite as real." It should be noted, however, that although it was easier to be a victim online, it was also easier to be aggressive and tell someone to "knock it off." This was especially true with middle-school girls, who often lacked the courage to speak up in face-to-face conversations.

In summary, there are some worrisome elements that arise when teens regularly use IM and social networking sites. There are also some positive, even exciting things that can happen only in a virtual environment. As parents contemplate how to manage the technology in their homes, it is helpful to think about the strengths and weaknesses of things like IM and social networking, considering how to come alongside young people as they navigate the technology that will become an inevitable part of their adult lives.

"Volunteering plays a valuable role in
shaping how youth learn to interact
with their community."

Teens Value Volunteerism

Corporation for National & Community Service

*The Corporation for National & Community Service encourages
community engagement through volunteerism. It surveyed over
three thousand young Americans for its 2005 report on youths
and community service, from which the following viewpoint is
excerpted. Based on the study, the corporation contends that the
majority of youths participated voluntarily in community service
projects in 2004. Not only did they make time to volunteer, but
many helped plan their project or reflected on their experience
afterward, the organization observes. Volunteerism is valuable to
young people, in the corporation's opinion, because it boosts self-
esteem, fosters a sense of community engagement, and leads to
better school performance.*

As you read, consider the following questions:

1. According to the Corporation for National & Community Service, how many youths volunteered in 2004 and
   for how many hours, collectively?

2. How did the study categorize regular, occasional, and episodic volunteers?
3. What three environments play formative roles in youth development, in the organization's view?

A t a time when many are worried that the United States is experiencing a general decline in civic and political engagement, volunteering appears particularly strong among today's [in 2005] young people. While volunteering is just one form of community involvement, research has shown that it is often connected to other forms of engagement, and, among youth, volunteering plays a valuable role in shaping how youth learn to interact with their community and develop the skills, values, and sense of empowerment necessary to become active citizens.

In an effort to better understand the attitudes and behaviors of young people in America around volunteering, service-learning and other forms of community involvement, the Corporation for National and Community Service, in collaboration with the U.S. Census Bureau and Independent Sector, conducted the Youth Volunteering and Civic Engagement Survey (the Youth Volunteering Survey), a national survey of American youth. Between January and March of 2005, 3,178 Americans between the ages of 12 and 18 were asked about their volunteer activities and experiences with school-based service-learning projects, as well as their involvement with school, family, religious congregations, and community associations.

The following report will highlight the state of youth volunteering and consider the relationship between youth volunteer behavior and three primary environments where youth form their social networks: family, religious organizations, and school. These social institutions play an essential role in connecting youth to volunteer opportunities and encouraging them to become engaged in service. Fostering environments that encourage volunteer activities is critical to creating a commitment to service and community involvement that will remain with them for their lifetime. Through this analysis, we look to build on existing research that has demonstrated that connections to the community and volunteering form a positive feedback loop, whereby opportunities provided to youth to engage with others leads to a greater sense of reciprocity and trust that in turn leads youth to develop a personal ethic of community engagement. . . .

A Large Number of Young Volunteers

According to the survey, the state of youth volunteering in America appears robust: an estimated 15.5 million teenagers participated in volunteer activities through a formal organization during 2004, contributing more than 1.3 billion hours of service. *That translates into a rate of 55 percent—more than one and a half times the adult rate of 29 percent* as established by the Census and Bureau of Labor Statistics' 2004 Current Population Survey figures, which used the same questions and definitions as the Youth Volunteering Survey.

Teens tend to serve fewer hours and with less regularity than their adult counterparts. For example, the study found that the typical youth volunteer contributes 29 hours of service each year, compared to 52 hours for the adult volunteer population.

Like other studies, this survey confirmed [that] the likelihood that young people will volunteer is related to their connections to the community through the social institutions of family, religious congregations, and schools. For example, the study found that:

- When compared to a youth with no family members who volunteer, a youth from a family where at least one parent volunteers is almost two times more likely to volunteer, and nearly three times more likely to volunteer on a regular basis.

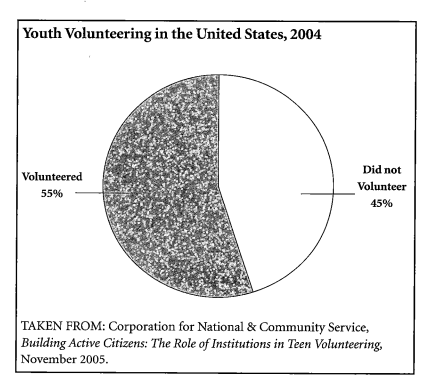

Youth Volunteering in the United States, 2004

Volunteered
55%

Did not
Volunteer
45%

TAKEN FROM: Corporation for National & Community Service,
Building Active Citizens: The Role of Institutions in Teen Volunteering,
November 2005.

- 64 percent of teenagers who attend religious services regularly also volunteer, compared to 41 percent among those youth who do not attend religious services at all.

- 38 percent of youth, an estimated 10.6 million teenagers, have engaged in community service as part of a school activity, and 65 percent of these youth were engaged in service-learning related activities, such as planning or reflecting on the service project.

- What's more, only 5 percent of youth attributed their volunteer activities to a school requirement.

- High school students are more likely to volunteer than junior high school students—58 percent compared to 49 percent, respectively.

Community Connections

Going beyond previous studies linking volunteering to individual and social characteristics, this analysis also looked at the frequency of youth volunteering, and at the relationship between social institutions and their level of volunteer commitment.

To aid in that analysis, the authors of the study categorized those who volunteered twelve or more weeks a year as "regular" volunteers; those who volunteered three to eleven weeks a year as "occasional" volunteers; and those who volunteered one or two weeks a year as "episodic" volunteers. Using these criteria the survey found that:

- 39 percent of the teenagers who volunteer are regular volunteers, compared with 55 percent of adult volunteers who fall in that category, while 35 percent of youth are occasional volunteers and 27 percent are episodic volunteers.

- The stronger the social ties, the more likely a teen is to be a regular volunteer:

    Youth with at least one parent who volunteers are nearly three times more likely to be regular volunteers than youth from non-volunteer families—33 percent and 11 percent, respectively.

    Youth who attend religious services regularly are nearly twice as likely to be regular volunteers as those who do not attend services.

    Students who report doing better in school are more likely to volunteer regularly than are students who do not do as well.

- High school students are more likely to be regular volunteers than are junior high school students—24 percent and 15 percent, respectively. . . .

To examine the possibility that school service requirements might be a factor in the high volunteering rate, youth were asked how they came to be involved with the organization with which they volunteered. We discovered that only 5 percent of youth reported that they became involved with the main organization with which they volunteer as the result of a school requirement.

Our study also found that youth tend to volunteer most often with three types of organizations: religious congregations, schools, and youth leadership organizations, which include such organizations as the Boy & Girl Scouts, the 4-H Club, Kiwanis (Key Club and Builders Club) and the National Honor Society. The majority of youth who volunteer, or 64 percent, reported that one of these three organizations was the main organization with which they volunteered. In addition, 74 percent of volunteers served with one or more of these organizations to at least some extent. Not only do these three types of organizations tend to provide opportunities for youth to volunteer, they are also important sites for the development of youth socialization and tend to have a high expectation for community service. . . .

Given our interest in examining volunteering as a learned social behavior, we wanted to explore some of the key social institutions that help to guide and shape youth development. We began by identifying three environments that play formative roles in youth development: family, religious institutions, and school. Not only are these environments where youth develop their identity and attitudes, they are also important areas where youth develop their social networks. Volunteering is an activity that has the potential to expand an individual's sense of community through interacting with others from different backgrounds. In this way, primary social institutions that encourage service, such as family, religious institutions, and schools, have the potential to foster in youth a sense of community that extends beyond their immediate circle.

We begin with the initial site where youth develop their identity, attitudes, and relationship to a community—their family.

Family and Volunteering

Youth development begins with the family, which has a formative impact on youth attitudes and behaviors. It is not surprising, therefore, to find that the volunteering habits of the family, particularly the parents, would have a significant impact on the volunteering habits of youth. Previous research has demonstrated that the parents' volunteering activities influences the likelihood that youth will volunteer during their childhood and later in adulthood. By volunteering, parents provide a role model for engaging with the larger community.

When looking at family volunteering, we created seven mutually exclusive and exhaustive categories. These categories differentiate between the immediate family, which consists of both parents and siblings, and the extended family, which consists of aunts, uncles, and grandparents. The Youth Volunteering Survey recorded information on these family members only. However, the survey did not record information on the number of members in each respondent's family.

Category 1: Both parents and at least one sibling volunteer

Category 2: Both parents but no siblings volunteer

Category 3: One parent and at least one sibling volunteer

Category 4: One parent volunteers

Category 5: Neither parent volunteers, but at least one sibling volunteers

Category 6: No one in their immediate family volunteers, but at least one member of the extended family volunteers

Category 7: No one in their immediate or extended family volunteers

The Youth Volunteering Survey asked youth about the volunteering habits not only of their parents, but also among their siblings, grandparents, aunts and uncles. We found that parents have the strongest relationship to teen volunteering, followed by the immediate family, and finally the extended family. The more volunteer role models that youth have, the more likely they are to volunteer and volunteer regularly. We found that, compared to a youth with no family members who volunteer, a youth from a family where at least one parent volunteers is almost two times more likely to volunteer, and nearly three times more likely to volunteer on a regular basis. Likewise, whereas 64 percent of nonvolunteers reported that no one in their family volunteers, only 14 percent of youth who have two parents and siblings who volunteer reported that they had not volunteered in the previous year. Of those youth with parents and siblings who volunteer, nearly half, or 47 percent, are also regular volunteers. . . .

Attendance at Religious Services and Volunteering

Respondents to the survey were asked how frequently they attended religious services in the past year, outside of weddings or funerals. Based on their responses, we found a strong correlation between the frequency with which respondents attend religious services and volunteering.

According to the survey, 62 percent of youth attend religious services to at least some extent, and 49 percent of youth are regular attendees—that is they attend religious services generally every week. The population of youth who regularly attend religious services are the most likely to volunteer, with an overall volunteering rate of 64 percent. This compares to 53 percent of those who said that they attend religious services infrequently and 41 percent of those who reported that they do not attend religious services at all. In addition, those who regularly attend religious services are nearly twice as likely to volunteer regularly than those who do not attend religious services at all.

While regular involvement in religious services appears to translate into a greater amount of involvement in volunteer activities, many of those volunteer activities are not taking place with the religious congregation. Among the respondents who regularly attend religious services, only 47 percent said that the main organization that they volunteer with is a religious congregation. The rest volunteer with an organization other than a religious congregation; 8 percent volunteer with a faith-based organization that is not a religious congregation, while the remaining youth, 45 percent, serve with a secular organization. This finding indicates that religious attendance may be part of a larger social network that provides youth with the opportunities and encouragement to engage in the community. Involvement with religious congregations may connect youth with volunteering opportunities, and it is also likely that the value placed on service in these organizations contributes to an expectation for youth to engage in volunteering and helps to instill in them an ethic of service that they carry with them into other areas of their lives.

School and Volunteering

School is a key area for youth socialization. Not only is it a place where youth begin to develop an identity apart from their family, it is also a context in which youth begin to develop a sense of a larger community to which they belong. In addition, previous research has shown that involvement in volunteering through schools, whether through community service or service-learning, can lead to improvements in self-esteem and academic achievement. In response to the overall decline in civic engagement among Americans, the past decade has seen a growing debate on the role that educational institutions should play in promoting civic education in schools.

Over the past twenty years, more schools have begun to recognize and arrange community service activities for their students. A national survey of school principals by the Department of Education in 1999 found that 46 percent of public high schools and 38 percent of public middle schools offer service-learning opportunities for their students, while 83 percent of high schools and 77 percent of middle schools organize community service opportunities. This compares to only 9 percent for service-learning opportunities and 27 percent for community service opportunities among public high schools in 1984, a sign that the majority of America's schools today place an emphasis on the value of service.

While some community service and service-learning activities through school are mandatory for students, school-based requirements represent a small percentage of volunteering engagement among youth. Only 5 percent of youth attributed their volunteering activities to a school requirement. In addition, while mandated community service may not have the same positive impacts as voluntary service, research has also demonstrated that youth benefit from organized planning and reflection of their service experience, such as occurs during participation in service-learning activities.

Respondents were asked whether they had ever performed any community service as part of a school activity or requirement. We found that 38 percent of youth, or approximately 10.6 million youth nationwide, have taken part in these kinds of activities. We also asked respondents who had engaged in this type of school-based service activity whether they had helped to plan the activity or write about and reflect on their service experience, both signs that they were engaged in service-learning activities. We found that 65 percent of those engaged in school-based service took part in one or both of these activities—36 percent, or 3.8 million participants, helped to plan their service project and 51 percent, or 5.4 million, wrote about or reflected on their service experience in class.

Periodical Bibliography

The following articles have been selected to supplement the diverse views presented in this chapter.

Tanzila Ahmed
"Don't Call Us Apathetic," *WireTap*, January 9, 2006. www.wiretapmag.org.

Howard Dukes
"Students Value Their Volunteer Work," *South Bend Tribune (IN)*, May 2, 2006.

Jeff Koopersmith
"Fickle Teens Dump Evangelical Lifestyle," *American Politics Journal*, April 2, 2007.

Richard Leyland
"Unwired: Prepare for the Next Generation," Silicon.com, October 10, 2006. http://management.silicon.com.

Janet Marshall
"Is This RE, Miss? It's Cool!" *ACT Now*, Summer 2004. www.christian-teachers.org.uk.

Scotty McLennan
"Doorways to Spirituality for Students," *Journal of College & Character*, November 2005.

Petaluma (CA) Argus-Courier
"Morals, Beliefs and Values: 101," March 7, 2007.

Caramie Schnell
"The Wired Generation," *Vail Trail*, October 4, 2006.

Christian Smith interviewed by Tony Jones
"Youth and Religion," Youth Specialties, 2005. www.youthspecialties.com.

Kate Tsubata
"A Youth's Year of Living Purposefully" *Washington Times*, September 4, 2006.

Adrienne Washington
"Young Voters Now Must Maintain Momentum," *Washington Times*, November 5, 2004.

Judy Woodruff
hosting *Online NewsHour*, "Young Voters Speak Out on Election-Year Issues, Politicians," October 25, 2006. www.pbs.org.

 **OPPOSING VIEWPOINTS® SERIES**

What Behaviors Do Young People Engage In?

Chapter Preface

Newspaper headlines and news programs regularly blare warnings about teens in crisis. Anyone who follows the reports, covering topics like youth gang involvement, eating habits, or risky driving, can find it difficult to keep such stories in perspective. Statistics conflict over whether young Americans are conducting themselves better than ever or more poorly than in the past. Accurately measuring youth behavior is difficult. For instance, researchers may depend on self reports and questionnaires on which youths can underreport or exaggerate their behavior. Other measures of teens' activities, such as crime rates, can also underestimate actual behavior. Statistics that show a drop in juvenile crime, for example, could merely reflect that young criminals are getting smarter about not getting caught. Contradictory figures regarding youth behaviors fuel debates between those who think young people today are doing well and those who believe their behavior has not improved.

According to some experts, young people are behaving better than those in the past and often better than the media portrays them. The Child Well-Being Index shows youths have been engaging in fewer risky behaviors over the since the mid-1990s. This data led Jeffrey Butts, who directs the youth justice program at the Urban Institute, to comment to the Associated Press, "Maybe we have the next 'greatest generation' coming along here." Teen pregnancy and drug use are two areas in which young people may be showing progress. National Vital Statistics Reports 2005 notes that the number of teens giving birth has fallen steadily since 1990. This may be due to more young people using birth control and more of them waiting to start having sex. Teen drug use statistics are improving as well. The 2006 Monitoring the Future survey discovered that alcohol and cocaine use among youths has declined since the 1990s, and marijuana use has decreased among tenth and twelfth graders for the fifth year in a row. Since the mid-1990s teen smoking has dropped off as well. Some commentators suggest that this means the actions of young Americans are not as unfavorable as many people assume.

However, warnings about teens and their bad behavior abound. A *Newsweek* cover in 1954 proclaimed, "Let's Face It: Our Teenagers Are Out of Control," and the sentiment remains among some juvenile experts and parents today. Donna Gaines, author of *Teenage Wasteland*, takes this view. She blames parents, school officials, and other adults for teens' poor conduct:

> Kids aren't thriving. . . . You're saying they're sub-literate. You're calling them burnouts, dirtbags, and losers. What are you really giving to them? You're neglecting them. You're starving them—emotionally, physically, psychologically— you're giving them no resources and then you're blaming them.

Those who support her view offer evidence that youth substance abuse and unprotected sex, among other behaviors, remain major problems. The September 2006 issue of *Journal of Adolescent Health*, for example, detailed risky sexual behavior among young people. Of fifteen- to nineteen-year-olds, 22 percent who had had at least one casual sex partner in the past three months and 19 percent who had had sex with only their main partner had not used a condom. Substance use remains a crisis among youths, too, argue mental health experts. Monitoring the Future discovered that prescription drug use by young people is lingering at a peak high. Furthermore, some 11 million teens in America drink alcohol in spite of laws prohibiting it. These numbers are upsetting to those who work to ensure the safety and wellbeing of youths.

Unprotected sex and substance abuse among young Americans are just a small segment of the debate over the years activities they engage in. Whether youth behavior is improving or worsening is the main controversy tackled by the authors in the next chapter, as well as the ramifications of young people's behaviors.

"Rapidly rising juvenile crime today will mean rapidly rising adult crime tomorrow."

Juvenile Crime Is on the Rise

Bradley Hope

In the following viewpoint Bradley Hope attests to a surge in youth crime in the United States involving such offenses as felony robbery, assault, murder, and grand larceny. At the same time, he maintains, there has been an increase in the number of juvenile arrests across the country's major cities as well as an upsurge in juvenile imprisonments in his city of New York. The soaring crime rate may be due to increased gang activity, fewer job opportunities, and a significant school dropout rate, according to authorities cited by Hope. A staff reporter for the New York Sun, *Hope writes frequently on crime.*

As you read, consider the following questions:

1. According to one of Hope's sources, what objects have been increasingly stolen in juvenile robberies?
2. How many juvenile delinquency filings were there in 2001, 2004, and 2005, in the author's assertion?

3. What were youths attempting to smuggle onto school grounds, according to New York City mayor Michael Bloomberg in the viewpoint?

Juveniles are getting arrested for felony robberies at a rapidly rising rate, the latest police statistics show. Some experts believe the data show a need for the city to focus more resources on after-school and work placement programs for residents under the age of 16.

About 6.7% more juveniles—nearly 90% of them boys—have been arrested for robbery this year [2006] through September 30 compared with the same period last year. There was an even more dramatic increase between 2004 and 2005, when juvenile arrests rose by 26.6%, to 2,814 from 2,222.

The New York Police Department's [NYPD's] deputy commissioner of strategic initiatives, Michael Farrell, said the rise starting in 2005 was due largely to an increase in the number of robberies of iPods, cellular phones, and other portable electronic devices.

Youth Crime in Major U.S. Cities

New York City has appeared to be immune to the more dire national crime trends over the last several years. While the FBI's uniform crime reports show violent crime rising about 2.3% nationally, New York's murder rate has increased only slightly, and other major crimes have dropped versus last year, CompStat [computerized statistics] reports show.

The latest data show that the city's juvenile population is more in line with problems seen in other major metropolitan cities, such as Washington, D.C., Minneapolis [MN], and Boston [MA]. The number of juveniles arrested for robbery in Boston increased by 54% between 2004 and 2005.

Police officials in those cities have said the number of juvenile arrests for robbery and assault have increased alongside gang activity and weapons possession. The NYPD recently testified at a city council hearing that the estimated number of gang members in the city has increased to 15,000 from 12,000.

While more modest than other cities, the rise in New York City is worrying, experts said. Juvenile crime is watched closely because spikes have sometimes preceded larger crime trends, the president of the Citizen's Crime Commission, Richard Aborn. said.

"This obviously is an area that the city needs to address," he said. "Rapidly rising juvenile crime today will mean rapidly rising adult crime tomorrow."

Statistics from other city agencies show that more juveniles are spending time in secure detention centers and being charged with juvenile delinquency.

Alongside a 13.7% increase in the number of juveniles admitted to secure facilities [in New York City] maintained by the Department of Juvenile Justice between fiscal 2005 and fiscal 2006, there have been 127 more instances of youth-on-youth assaults, a 39.1% increase. The number of juvenile delinquency filings in the Family Court Division rose to 6,259 in 2005 from 5,379 in 2004. There were 4,828 filings in 2001, according to data acquired from the city's law department.

A community re-entry coordinator at the Children's Aid Society, Lance Johnsonn, said the thin job market and reduced funding for summer youth programs are pushing the robbery rates higher.

"When it's hard to get a job, they'll get caught up on a robbery charge," he said. "The iPods and cell phones, those are easy things to sell on the street."

Allan Luks, the executive director of a youth support organization, Big Brothers, Big Sisters, said the rising crime rate for youths also linked up with the high school dropout rate in the city.

"Social disconnectedness is affecting our entire society," he said. "For poor youths, with the very significantly high dropout rate, single-parent homes, onslaught of the media, televi-

Blame the Juvenile Justice System for Increasing Youth Crime

I have seen firsthand the devastating effects of an ineffective juvenile justice system. One of the last cases I prosecuted as United States attorney was a carjacking case out of Gainesville, Florida. Five persons, including one 19-year-old, two 18-year-olds and two 14-year-olds, shot a 72-year-old man in Ocala and later abducted a 19-year-old college student in Gainesville. As it turned out, the defendants collectively had numerous prior juvenile arrests for such offenses as attempted first-degree murder, aggravated assault, and assault and battery, and one of the juveniles had dozens of prior auto theft arrests in his background. Despite these arrests, the juvenile displayed a defiant attitude, telling me that he had never served a day in jail and that "you can't touch me." . . .

In his [summer of 1997] *Policy Review* article, [Eugene] Methvin cited numerous studies confirming that society's failure to take punitive action in dealing with first-time youthful offenders is a primary factor contributing to the development of habitual criminals. As Mr. Methvin noted, "a troublesome youngster typically has ten or 12 contacts with the criminal-justice system and many more undiscovered offenses before he ever receives any formal 'adjudication,' or finding of guilt, from a judge. He quickly concludes that he will never face any serious consequences for his delinquency." Our experience in Florida clearly bears this out.

Kenneth W. Sukhia, Putting Consequences Back into Juvenile Justice at the Federal, State, and Local Levels, *Hearing before the Subcommittee on Crime of the Committee on the Judiciary House of Representatives, March 10 and 11, 1999.*

sion, and movies . . . this is a generation where you worry first and foremost about yourself. When you have all that, you are left with the values of the street."

Addressing the Problem of Juvenile Crime

Gang involvement, he said, is a way for youths to feel needed and a sense of belonging. His organization tries to show troubled youths that involvement with greater society can give the same things, he said.

While robberies spiral higher for juveniles, the number of juvenile arrests for murder has increased to 32 from 28 between 2004 and 2005. Arrests for rape, burglary, grand larceny auto, and assault have decreased. Grand larcenies increased to 492 in 2005 from 380 in 2004.

[New York City] mayor [Michael] Bloomberg said in a radio interview on 1010 WINS in October that the rising juvenile crime rate was "worrisome."

"That's why you focus on the schools," he said. He said he had heard stories from officials that youths were trying to smuggle brass knuckles, handguns, and box cutters onto school grounds.

The mayor touted statistics showing that citywide crime in schools was down 7% since the start of the impact program [to increase school security] in April 2003.

The director of the New School's Center for City Affairs, Andrew White, said the city needs to focus more on social welfare programs for youths.

"It's a little disturbing to me that we don't have a better way of dealing with younger teens as they are struggling in schools and getting ready to drop out," he said.

"Americans are experiencing the sharpest decline in teen crime in modern history."

Juvenile Crime Is Decreasing

Frank Greve

Frank Greve claims in the following viewpoint that crime committed by minors is at a remarkable low. Arrests for homicide, robbery, rape, and aggravated assault have all dropped off, despite predictions by juvenile criminologists of the 1990s that violent crime would double among youths. He credits several factors, including the decline of the crack market, the mentoring of youth, and the imprisonment of more adult criminals, for this decline. Frank Greve, a national correspondent of the Washington Bureau, earned a George Polk Award for journalism.

As you read, consider the following questions:

1. What does James Rieland tell new prosecutors, according to the author?
2. In Franklin Zimring's contention, what is the bad news about juvenile crime?
3. What are the five theories that explain the drop in teen crime, as Greve puts it?

A new generation of brutal and remorseless teens was about to savage the nation, leading authorities on juvenile crime warned a decade ago [in 1996]. Millions of Americans believed them.

Conservative criminologist John Dilulio called the fearsome horde "super-predators." He estimated that they'd number nearly 200,000 by now. Even Attorney General Janet Reno foresaw violent crime doubling among kids.

It never happened. Instead, Americans are experiencing the sharpest decline in teen crime in modern history. Schools today are as safe as they were in the 1960s, according to Justice Department figures. Juvenile homicide arrests are down from 3,800 annually to fewer than 1,000, and only a handful of those homicides occur in schools. Arrest rates for robbery, rape and aggravated assault are off a third since 1980 for children aged 10–18, according to the Justice Department's 2006 *National Report on Juvenile Offenders and Victims*, due out [in March 2006].

"Kids now are less violent than you were," James Rieland, the director of juvenile court services in Pittsburgh's Allegheny County, tells new prosecutors.

Today, criminologists say the real question is what went right in the long period of relative peace that dawned in the mid-'90s. Their hope is to prolong it, or at least know what works the next time juvenile crime goes up.

How the Trend Leveled Off

Teen-crime declines leveled off in 2002 and 2003, the latest years for which solid numbers are available. Simple assaults are up, especially among girls, according to the upcoming Justice Department report, and teen drug arrests, while off their peaks, never fell as far as violent and property crimes. That's the bad news, said criminologist Franklin Zimring of the University of California-Berkeley School of Law. "The good news," he added, "is that juvenile crime overall is staying at the lowest level it's been in 36 years."

The rise and fall of crack cocaine was the biggest factor, most juvenile-crime experts agree. Others include an inner-city influx of relatively peaceable Latino families, a thriving economy, improved strategies for dealing with real and potential delinquents, more adult imprisonment, smarter policing and better school-parent partnerships.

According to criminologist Alfred Blumstein of Carnegie Mellon University in Pittsburgh, teen crime's decline is largely the downside of a rise that started in the mid-80s when kids took over drug gangs from adult dealers who'd been imprisoned under toughened state and federal laws. The teens needed guns "because crack was a street market and you had to protect yourself," Blumstein said. "And they didn't have the restraint that older folks do."

It helped that crack's street price dropped in the mid-'90s, according to economist Steven Levitt, the author of the best seller *Freakonomics*, which includes an examination of teen crime's decline.

No surprise: The sharpest drops in teen crime since 1993 were among black males, who once dominated crack sales.

But crack's fade is just part of the story, because teen crime also fell sharply in suburbs where crack was scarce and in rural communities where there was none.

Most of those areas saw a dramatic surge in school security, mainly after the Columbine High School shootings in Littleton, Colo., in April 1999. That's long after teen crime started dropping, so the question is whether school security upgrades are keeping it down.

Explaining the Decline

Probably more important than tighter school security, criminologists said, were these factors:

Good economic times. In the decade of economic expansion that ended in 2000, the number of older teens who were neither in school nor at full-time jobs dropped by nearly a

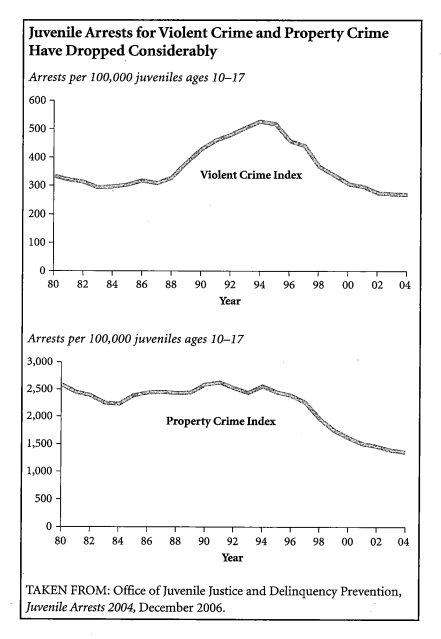

Juvenile Arrests for Violent Crime and Property Crime Have Dropped Considerably

Arrests per 100,000 juveniles ages 10–17

Violent Crime Index

Arrests per 100,000 juveniles ages 10–17

Property Crime Index

TAKEN FROM: Office of Juvenile Justice and Delinquency Prevention, *Juvenile Arrests 2004,* December 2006.

third, according to the U.S. Bureau of Labor Statistics. Prosperity, in other words, gave teens more and better options to crime.

Population shifts. The Latino population in central cities swelled as teen crime declined, according to Jeff Roth, a University of Pennsylvania criminologist. Their influx, Roth said, brought more intact families, strong values, higher religious participation—and lower crime rates. At the same time, many of the black families they replaced moved to suburbs where poverty was less concentrated. "Kids once confined to the inner city started seeing lifestyles other than the street," Roth said.

Learning what works. Criminologists decided in the '90s to track what worked and what didn't in dealing with teen crime. Boot camps didn't work, they found. Nor did trying juveniles in adult courts. Big Brother and Big Sister mentoring worked. Foster care for delinquents worked better than lock-ups if foster parents were well trained and the goal was to return the delinquents to well-coached biological parents. Suspending delinquent kids from school or leaving them back didn't work. One happy surprise: They found that if one parent is strong and consistent, the second isn't missed when it comes to preventing delinquency.

Imprisoning adults. The incarceration rate rose from 1 per 1,000 adults to 4 from the '80s to today, and there are many critics of the causes of that increase. But Blumstein, who's among them, and others think that jailing more adults sharply reduced the number of teens who commit crimes with adult accomplices.

Abortion. Economist Levitt attributes teen crime's sharp drop to a reduction in unwanted children, which began with the Supreme Court's *Roe v. Wade* decision in 1973. Criminologist Zimring, among others, thinks it contributed but isn't as big a factor as Levitt argues.

"Many young people . . . simply do not consider oral sex to be as significant as their parents' generation does."

More Youths Are Engaging in Oral Sex

Laura Sessions Stepp

In the viewpoint that follows, Laura Sessions Stepp provides evidence of an oral sex trend among teenagers. A 2005 national survey, she maintains, confirms that more than half of fifteen- to nineteen-year-olds have had oral sex and that the number of girls who have received oral sex is equal to that of boys. In Stepp's contention, these statistics illustrate that youths consider oral sex to be more socially acceptable—and mistakenly believe it is safer—than intercourse. The study further reveals that as many girls have casual sex as boys, she asserts. Stepp wrote Unhooked: How Young Women Pursue Sex, Delay Love, and Lose at Both.

As you read, consider the following questions:

1. According to Stepp, what percent of eighteen- and nineteen-year-olds have had oral sex?

2. How does James Wagoner explain his assertion that the survey reflects a major social transition?

3. What are the risks of oral sex, in the author's view?

Slightly more than half of American teenagers ages 15 to 19 have engaged in oral sex, with females and males reporting similar levels of experience, according to the most comprehensive national survey of sexual behaviors ever released by the federal government.

The report released yesterday [September 15, 2005] by the National Center for Health Statistics shows that the proportion increases with age to about 70 percent of all 18- and 19-year-olds. That figure is considerably higher for those who also have engaged in intercourse.

The Findings Are Shocking

Several leaders of organizations that study or work with youth expressed surprise at the level of girls' participation. "You assume that females are more likely to give, males more likely to receive," said Jennifer Manlove, who directs fertility research for the organization Child Trends. "We were surprised that the percentages were similar."

A report by the center nine months ago, based on the same survey, showed that slightly more girls than boys have intercourse before they turn 20. In addition, other national data indicate that the proportion of high school girls who have one-night stands, as well as nonromantic sexual relationships, equals boys.

"This is a point of major social transition," James Wagoner, president of Advocates for Youth, a reproductive health organization, said yesterday [September 15, 2005]. "The data are now coming out and roiling the idea that boys are the hunters and young girls are the prey. It absolutely defies the stereotype."

Joe McIllhaney Jr., chairman of the Medical Institute for Sexual Health, said the new data confirm trends he has seen as a physician, but he has doubts about some of Wagoner's conclusions. "I question how much girls enjoy" oral sex, he said. "I'd like to know a whole lot more about the pressure boys put on girls."

A Different Generation

The data also underscore the fact that many young people—particularly those from middle- and upper-income white families—simply do not consider oral sex to be as significant as their parents' generation does. "Oral sex is far less intimate than intercourse. It's a different kind of relationship," said Claire Brindis, professor of pediatrics at the University of California at San Francisco. "At 50 percent, we're talking about a major social norm. It's part of kids' lives."

Bill Albert, communications director for the National Campaign to Prevent Teen Pregnancy, put the generational difference this way: "We used to talk about sex in terms of first base, second base and so on. Oral sex was maybe in the dugout." The news for parents, he said, is that they must broaden the discussions they have with their children about sex and be more specific. "If they want their teens to abstain from sex, they need to say exactly what they want their kids to abstain from."

The entire survey, administered in 2002 and 2003, includes a variety of findings about sexual behaviors among 15-to 44-year-olds. For example, almost 11 percent of young women ages 15 to 19 said they had had some kind of sexual experience with a female partner, a figure that also held true for 15-to-44-year-old women in general. Proportions of men reporting same-sex activities were lower.

The findings on oral sex among teens are sure to stir debate over abstinence-only sex education. Supporters of such programs say they have resulted in young people delaying intercourse, but opponents say they also have led young people to substitute other behaviors, especially fellatio and cunnilin-

Oral Sex Is Not Without Risks

"Young adolescents are perceiving that oral sex is less risky than vaginal sex in terms of health risks—STDs, pregnancy, and HIV," [researcher Bonnie L.] Halpern-Felsher says. "They also see oral sex as having fewer social and emotional risks. They think they are less likely to feel guilty, to get in trouble, to have a bad reputation, or to have a relationship problem. They also feel oral sex is more acceptable. They think more teens are having it, and that it is OK in the context of both a dating and nondating relationship—a one-night stand in our terms."

One finding that worries Halpern-Felsher is that a small but significant proportion of teens think oral sex carries zero physical risk. Fourteen percent of teens said there was zero risk of getting HIV from oral sex, and 13% said the behavior carried zero risk of transmitting chlamydia. Only 1% and 2%, respectively, thought vaginal sex carried zero risk of HIV or chlamydia infection. Experts say there is no doubt that oral sex can transmit virtually any sexually transmitted disease—including HIV and chlamydia.

Daniel J. DeNoon,
"1 in 5 Young Teens Report Having Tried Oral Sex,"
Web MD, *April 9, 2007. www.WebMD.com.*

gus. The new data tend to support this view, showing that nearly one in four virgin teens has engaged in oral sex.

The Risks

Many teenagers have fully accepted the idea that postponing intercourse is a good thing to do, Brindis said. When they weigh the advantages and disadvantages of intercourse vs. other forms of sex, they decide that they are far more at risk with intercourse, because of possible pregnancy and the greater risk of infection. Teens also consider oral sex more acceptable in their peer group than vaginal sex.

"They're very smart about this issue," Brindis said, "but they may not have been given a strong enough message about the risks of oral sex. Maybe we need to do a better job of showing them they need to use condoms." Oral sex has been associated in clinical studies with several infections, including gonorrhea, syphilis, herpes and the human papillomavirus, which has been linked to cervical cancer. Condoms and other forms of contraception can be used to decrease the health risks of oral sex, but few teens use them.

"If a substantial number of young people are having oral sex, as these numbers indicate, this is a big concern," said Kristin Moore, president of Child Trends, which analyzed the center's most recent findings.

> *"The teenage fellatio craze exists mainly among adults."*

Claims that More Youths Are Having Oral Sex Are Exaggerated

Cathy Young

In the following viewpoint Cathy Young debunks claims that teens are engaging in oral sex at rates like never before. Widespread stories about parties where boys receive oral sex from several girls are nothing more than unsubstantiated rumors, she avers. Furthermore, asserts Young, surveys on which some of these claims are based may not be accurate and do not ask whether the teens who engage in oral sex are having one-night stands or are in committed relationships. Young is an author and a contributing editor of Reason, *a libertarian magazine.*

As you read, consider the following questions:

1. How does Young respond to Michelle Burford's assertion that rainbow parties are common?
2. What evidence does the author provide to support her notion that the number of teens who engage in oral sex has remained constant?

Cathy Young, "The Great Fellatio Scare," *Reason*, May 2006. Copyright © 2006 by Reason Foundation, 3415 S. Sepulveda Blvd., Suite 400, Los Angeles, CA 90034, www.reason.com. Reproduced by permission.

3. What leads the author to conclude that a lot of teens surveyed about oral sex were being dishonest?

The teenage oral sex panic began in the late 1990s. It is in some ways a part of the Clinton legacy—more specifically, the Clinton-Lewinsky legacy. [In 1998 President Bill Clinton faced impeachment for lying about having received oral sex from White House intern Monica Lewinsky.] It was Clinton's most famous line ("I did not have sexual relations with that woman, Miss Lewinsky") and the subsequent debate on whether receiving oral sex qualified as "sexual relations" that produced the apparently shocking disclosure that a lot of teenagers were not only engaging in oral sex but regarding it as not quite sex.

Worse: According to press accounts, America's young Monicas weren't just having oral sex; they were having it in circumstances that would raise Hugh Hefner's eyebrows. In July 1998, *The Washington Post* ran a front-page story with the headline, "Parents Are Alarmed by an Unsettling New Fad in Middle Schools: Oral Sex."

Scandalous, Unsubstantiated Stories

Its main example was a scandal in an Arlington, Virginia, school, where a group of eighth-graders would get together for parties at which boys and girls paired off for sexual activities that eventually progressed from petting to oral sex. There were also a couple reported instances of public fellatio, on a school bus and in a hallway, that reached school authorities "through the student grapevine."

From here, it was only a short step to tales of "rainbow parties" where several girls wearing different colors of lipstick would take turns servicing a boy until their lipstick traces formed a "rainbow" of rings. In 2003, this peril was explored by Oprah herself, with the help of *O* magazine feature writer Michelle Burford, who interviewed 50 girls, some as young as

9, and painted a frightening picture of kiddie debauchery. "Are rainbow parties pretty common?" inquired a rapt Oprah, to which Burford replied, "I think so. At least among the 50 girls that I talked to ... this was pervasive."

Burford did not say whether the girls had told her they themselves had attended such parties, or if they had simply heard rumors. Nor was any proof produced of what was actually said in those interviews.

All these stories invariably depicted the oral sex as almost entirely one-sided, with girls giving and boys receiving. "One more opportunity for male satisfaction and female degradation in the name of adolescent sexual curiosity," harrumphed *Baltimore Sun* columnist Susan Reimer. In this familiar script, feminists saw girls as victims of male dominance, while conservatives blamed feminists and Clinton, whose bad example supposedly sent kids the message that fellatio was OK.

Now the "rainbow party" tale—which has never been substantiated and may well have originated with that *Washington Post* story—has become the subject of a novel, Paul Ruditis' *The Rainbow Party*, published last summer by Simon Pulse, a young adult division of Simon & Schuster. While conservatives have widely denounced the book as yet another excrescence of our licentious culture, its message actually seems to be one of almost old-fashioned moralism: The girl who plans the party is humiliated when hardly anyone shows up, then punished with a gonorrhea infection to boot.

Overreactions

Ruditis' novel has prompted a new round of hand wringing. On the Fox News Channel's *Hannity & Colmes*, radio psychologist Judy Kuriansky asserted that teenagers had been telling her about rainbow parties for years on her show, and assured the shocked hosts that yes, those parties really were going on. "Unbelievable," sputtered Sean Hannity.

In Janitors' Closets, Libraries, and Stairwells

The first time I heard a mother of girls talk about the teenage oral-sex craze, I made her cry. The story she told me—about a bar mitzvah dinner dance on the North Shore of Chicago [IL], where the girls serviced all the boys on the chartered bus from the temple to the reception hall—was so preposterous that I burst out laughing. The thought of thirteen-year-old girls in party dresses performing a sex act once considered the province of prostitutes (we are talking here about the on-your-knees variety given to a series of near strangers) was so ludicrous that all I could do was giggle.

It was as though I had taken lightly the news that a pedophile had moved into my friend's neighborhood. It was as though I had laughed about a leukemia cluster or a lethal stretch of freeway. I apologized profusely; I told her I hadn't known.

The moms in my set are convinced—they're certain; they know for a *fact*—that all over the city, in the very best schools, in the nicest families, in the leafiest neighborhoods, twelve- and thirteen-year-old girls are performing oral sex on as many boys as they can. They're ducking into janitors' closets between classes to do it; they're doing it on school buses, and in bathrooms, libraries, and stairwells. They're making bar mitzvah presents of the act, and performing it at "train parties": boys lined up on one side of the room, girls working their way down the row.

Caitlin Flanagan, Atlantic Monthly,
January–February 2006.

Unbelievable, indeed. For one, as Caitlin Flanagan points out in a lengthy review essay in *The Atlantic*, the different colors of lipstick would almost inevitably smear and destroy the supposedly sought-after rainbow effect. Besides, a boy would have to be a sexual superathlete to complete the circuit. The "current oral-sex hysteria," Flanagan writes, "requires believing that a boy could be serviced at the school-bus train party— receiving oral sex from ten or fifteen girls, one after another— and then zip his fly and head off to homeroom, first stopping in the stairwell for a quickie to tide him over until math."

Unfortunately, while Flanagan—who has recently drawn attention with her tart, often thoughtful critiques of feminism—starts on a skeptical note, she turns around about a third of the way into her sprawling, nearly 9,000-word tract and succumbs to the hysteria. She dismisses the tales of orgies and rampant anonymous blowjobs as nonsense, noting that she has been able to find only one verified account of a girl performing oral sex on multiple boys at a party. Yet she thinks the reality is bad enough.

"We've made a world for our girls in which the pornography industry has become increasingly mainstream," Flanagan writes, "in which Planned Parenthood's response to the oral-sex craze has been to set up a help line, in which the forces of feminism have worked relentlessly to erode the patriarchy— which, despite its manifold evils, held that providing for the sexual safety of young girls was among its primary reasons for existence. And here are America's girls: experienced beyond their years, lacking any clear message from the adult community about the importance of protecting their modesty, adrift in one of the most explicitly sexualized cultures in the history of the world. Here are America's girls: on their knees."

Counterintuitive Findings

What is the basis for this Wendy Shalit-style outburst? A study by the National Center for Health Statistics and the Centers for Disease Control and Prevention, released in September 2005, found that 25 percent of 15-year-old girls and half of 17-year-olds had engaged in oral sex. While the survey did not include children under 15, the report noted that in a survey several months earlier, only 4 percent of adolescents 13 to 14 years old said they'd had oral sex. (Did any of this represent an increase from the past? Probably not: A Child Trends analysis of data from surveys of unmarried males ages 15 to 19 in 1995 and 2002 found no significant changes in reported rates of oral sex experience.)

While Flanagan talks about sex "outside of romantic relationships," the September 2005 study said nothing about the context in which these activities took place—casual encounters or steady dating.

The study did say something about one aspect of the alleged oral sex craze, something that contradicts conventional wisdom. Girls and boys, it turns out, are about equally likely to give and to receive. Actually, at least among younger adolescents, boys overall reported more oral sex experience than girls, but both boys and girls were more likely to report receiving oral sex than giving it—which suggests a lot of respondents are fibbing.

This finding was so counterintuitive that some "experts" chose to disbelieve it: Joe McIllhaney Jr., chairman of the Medical Institute for Sexual Health, told *The Washington Post* he doubted that girls were really enjoying oral sex: "I'd like to know a whole lot more about the pressure boys put on girls." Others, such as James Wagoner of the reproductive health organization Advocates for Youth, argued that the new data subverted the stereotype of boys as predators and girls as prey.

How does Flanagan deal with this information? By refusing to deal with it. Throughout the article, she assumes girls are only the givers, referring to "this strange new preference for unreciprocated oral sex" and even speculating that girls, ill-served by our modesty-unfriendly culture, have taken to giving oral sex in order to keep their own sexuality protected from male encroachments. (Boys, Flanagan adds, aren't vulnerable to the emotional repercussions of sex the way girls are, so as a mother of boys she has little personal concern about the oral peril.)

Are some kids having sex too soon, and with too many partners, for their own emotional and physical well-being? Almost certainly. But the majority do not inhabit the sexual jungle of worried adults' imaginations. The teenage fellatio craze exists mainly among adults. To those in the audience who are not worried parents, it provides both sexual and moralistic thrills; it plays both to the prurient fascination with teenage girls gone wild and to the paternalistic stereotype of girls as victims. It does very little to help either adolescents or their parents deal with the real problems of growing up.

> "From elementary classrooms to univer-
> sity halls, it's a generation—born 1982
> and after—[predicted to become] a po-
> litical and social powerhouse."

American Kids Are Regularly Taking Initiative

Joann Klimkiewicz

According to Joann Klimkiewicz in the following viewpoint, U.S. youths are more zealously socially engaged than ever before. In support of her assertion, she profiles adolescents who have—on their own accord—organized car washes, counted pennies for penny drives, arranged bake sales, and raised money for homeless shelters. The young generation, in her view, is demonstrating impressive maturity and eagerness to make a difference in the world. Klimkiewicz, a staff writer for Hartford Courant, *often writes on culture and lifestyle.*

As you read, consider the following questions:

1. What events have shaped the lives of young Americans, as Klimkiewicz puts it?
2. According to the author, what does David Shortell plan to do with his bar mitzvah money?

3. How does the author describe the life of Giovannie Mendez?

All summer long [in 2005], Devon Aldave wanted to organize a car wash in his West Hartford [CT] neighborhood. "Just for fun," the 8-year-old says with a shrug when asked to explain. But, as do many childhood impulses, the notion faded with the summer.

Then came Hurricane Katrina.

"I saw the kids on TV that were hurting because of Katrina, and I was sad," Devon says. "And I thought maybe we could do the car wash to raise money for them."

With his younger brothers and friends in tow, Devon soaped and sprayed his way on a recent Saturday afternoon to $241, which he donated to the American Red Cross.

It all left Lisa Aldave a proud mother—and very much in awe of the pint-size patrons.

"When I was growing up, all the fundraisers we had were strictly for school teams or the organizations we were attached to," says Aldave, 37. "It wasn't about philanthropy. I don't think we grew up with that mindset.

"This was something they took and truly did on their own."

Student-driven Katrina relief efforts have cropped up in schools and youth groups across the country. They're selling Mardi Gras beads and T-shirts during recess, hosting street-corner bake sales and lemonade stands—all with an eagerness that has parents and teachers taking notice.

And yet, it's not that surprising. This is the same group of kids who showed equal zeal taking on tsunami relief efforts last December [2004], the same kids who stack bunches of cause-related rubber bracelets around their ankles and wrists. They're setting record numbers for volunteerism and, scholars say, proving to be one of the most socially engaged generations in recent history.

And from elementary classrooms to university halls, it's a generation—born 1982 and after—that they predict will go on to be a political and social powerhouse.

Katrina Reveals Another Side of Youths

"This is an amazing generation of young people, and nobody knows it," says Steve Culbertson, president of Youth Service America, a Washington-based international nonprofit outfit. "And I think these hurricane-relief efforts are really putting it on the table. Just as [Katrina] revealed some of the sadder sides of life, it's also revealed this is the greatest generation of young kids that we've ever had in this country."

Lazy. Angst-ridden. Distracted. Each generation laments the one behind them. But the string of adjectives just doesn't apply to this group of American youth when taken as a whole, Culbertson says.

Their childhoods were shaped by the panic of a new millennium followed by the unprecedented tragedy of the [September 11,] 2001 terrorist attacks. A war in Afghanistan followed. Another in Iraq. And now news of natural disasters dominates the airwaves.

It's a profound mixture that seeps into their consciousness, speaking at once to the frailty of humanity and its strength to overcome.

At the Smith School of Science, Math & Technology in West Hartford, teacher Lauren Worley has seen this first-hand.

The hurricane was the subject on everyone's lips when the school year began. Worley wanted to encourage the students to help and proposed they scour their homes for loose change to donate to the relief efforts. Three weeks and umpteen jars of pennies later, the students raised $1,606.69—presenting the Red Cross with a check for that amount last week [in September 2005].

"I knew that if you give them the opportunity to do something, they take it and go with it," Worley says. "Somewhere

Teens Believe They Can Make an Impact

Nearly eight in ten teens (78%) believe people their age can create positive change in their communities, seven in ten teens (69%) believe they personally can make a positive change in their community, and more than six in ten teens (64%) believe people their age have good ideas about how to help the community.

Most teens choose to get involved in the community because it makes them feel good (68%), it is fun (67%) and it is the right thing to do (65%). . . .

The survey also found that teens who have participated in community service activities are more likely than those who have not to believe people their age can make a positive change in their community (89% vs. 69%), more likely to believe people their age can make an impact on the political system (48% vs. 34%), and are twice as likely to make mostly A's in school (34% vs. 17%).

HarrisInteractive, "Study Shows Teens' Top Ten Causes, Readiness to Get Involved and Make a Difference," August 27, 2001. www.harrisinteractive.com.

along the lines, they learned that when something like this happens, you help people when they need it."

That's what had fifth-graders Tatiana Smith and Sarah Smith (they are not related, but are very good friends, they say) trading sunny recesses for a half-hour of coin-counting nearly every day of the penny drive.

They've joined about 25 students who volunteered over the weeks to count and roll coins. There was no nudging, Worley says, no coaxing with rewards. They get no respite from a math lesson, no extra credit.

When asked why, Tatiana neatly, methodically stacked pennies as she described the devastation she's seen on television.

"They've been saying it's really bad. Everyday when I turn on the TV, it's [Hurricanes] Katrina and Rita," she says. "We have a home, and we can ride our bikes and scooters. We have a comfortable bed to sleep in and clothes to wear. They don't."

Fundraising for Good Causes

Seeing the images of devastation, of families washed from their homes, it's touched these kids deeper than some might guess.

It had Manuel Martinez unable to sleep the night before he and his schoolmates at McDonough Elementary School in Hartford hosted a bake sale for Katrina relief. And, he says, he was just so excited to be raising money to help, he nervously checked to make sure his mother bought the cake mix for the goodies he planned to contribute.

"They've got no place to go. We have so much, and they have so little now. Their homes are destroyed, and they have nothing," says Manuel, 11, who, with his peers, raised $200.

But it's not just about hurricane relief and fundraisers. These students are showing impressive maturity as they take to service projects and talk of opening themselves to worlds outside their own.

Two years ago, David Shortell's mother told him they'd be taking a two-week trip to Nicaragua with a Sister Cities program. This would be no Disneyland vacation. They'd be touring one of the poorest countries in the world, experiencing how families there live, extend some help if they could. But David didn't grumble. In fact, he was intrigued.

"When I came back, I was like, wow. I have a lot of things I take for granted," says David, 13.

So when it comes time for his bar mitzvah this month, David says he'll give a chunk of his gift money to a cause in Nicaragua. He'd like to help buy new musical supplies for a local band he met in San Ramon.

"It's like, I'm not going to go to the mall and spend it all. I gained so much from that experience, and I had to give something back," says David, who is also active with a youth volunteer group at his West Hartford temple.

In the last decade, volunteerism among youngsters has risen dramatically. In 1989, 66 percent of university freshman reported doing volunteer work in their last year of high school. That number jumped to 83 percent in 2003, according to a national study conducted annually by UCLA's Higher Education Research Institute.

Skeptics may attribute that to résumé-padding, college-bound students looking to stand out.

But 30 percent of young adults say they volunteer because they are asked, and 24 percent because it makes them feel good, according to the Center for Democracy & Citizenship. Eight percent concede they do it to build their résumés.

For Giovannie Mendez, organizing a holiday dinner and gift drive for a trio of homeless shelters last year had nothing to do with résumés.

"I went through it," says Mendez, 19, of Hartford, who was shuffled around foster homes, residential facilities and homeless shelters since he was 8. When he arrived for his first semester at Morris Brown College in Atlanta [GA] last year, he was moved when he learned of the extent of poverty in the city.

He and a core of five other students raised more than $1,000 to pull off a party that gave about 50 families a respite from the shelter, a hearty meal and holiday presents.

It's an event he continues at the campus and one he is considering bringing to Capital Community College, where he has since transferred.

"The gap between the haves and the have-nots is just getting so much bigger," Mendez says.

How does he think older generations perceive his own?

"That all we think about is ourselves, about going out to the clubs. That we're lazy," he says.

And the reality?

"Oh my gosh, no, we're so not lazy," says Giovannie, who, aside from receiving some state aid, is putting himself through school. "I wish I could be lazy sometimes."

The Rise of the Millennials

So what is all this do-gooding about? Are today's youth being prodded by adults or are they actually taking their own initiative?

Culbertson says students are learning the importance of volunteerism early on, with many schools requiring service projects for graduation. There's less talk of youth being the "future and hope of tomorrow," he says, and more focus on the valuable resources to societal change that they are now.

And a lot of credit, he says, can be given to their baby-boomer parents.

"These are parents who grew up during [the war in] Vietnam," Culbertson says. "And they have really high expectations of their children to be active community members."

And it's all been predicted, along with this generation's drop in drug and alcohol use and in teen pregnancy.

Neil Howe and William Strauss have written several books on generational history, their most recent being *Millennials Rising: The Next Generation*.

Using their theory that the generations follow a rhythmic pattern of characteristics—responding to global, domestic and economic conditions—they predicted that the Millennials, the name for the generation beginning with the Class of 2000, would be "poised to define the 21st Century in much the same way as the G.I.s defined the 20th."

From the snapshot Worley has gotten with her West Hartford students' penny drive, she's equally optimistic.

"This is an amazing bunch of kids," she says. "If in a few weeks they came up with more than $1,500—if that's how they carry on the rest of their lives, I think we're all going to be better off."

> *"Maybe every generation of kids has wanted to take it easy, but until the past few decades students were not allowed to get away with it."*

American Kids Are Unmotivated

Patrick Welsh

Patrick Welsh teaches English at T.C. Williams High School in Alexandria, Virginia. In the following viewpoint he charges that most of his American students lack motivation, self-discipline, and work ethic, unlike immigrant students, who he says work hard in school. In his experience, young Americans blame their teachers, not themselves, for the bad grades they receive when they do not put effort into their work. It is up to parents and the youths themselves to foster a sense of ambition and motivation, Welsh insists.

As you read, consider the following questions:

1. What were the conclusions of the University of Pennsylvania researchers, according to Welsh?
2. American students say that their performance in math depends on what factors, in the author's words?

Patrick Welsh, "For Once, Blame the Student," *USA Today*, March 8, 2006, p. 11A. Copyright 2006 *USA Today*. Reproduced by permission of the author.

3. What two things does the author say have turned into minimum-competency requirements?

Failure in the classroom is often tied to lack of funding, poor teachers or other ills. Here's a thought: Maybe it's the failed work ethic of today's kids. That's what I'm seeing in my school. Until reformers see this reality, little will change.

Last month, as I averaged the second-quarter grades for my senior English classes at T.C. Williams High School in Alexandria, Va., the same familiar pattern leapt out at me.

Kids who had emigrated from foreign countries—such as Shewit Giovanni from Ethiopia, Farah Ali from Guyana and Edgar Awumey from Ghana—often aced every test, while many of their U.S.-born classmates from upper-class homes with highly educated parents had a string of C's and D's.

As one would expect, the middle-class American kids usually had higher SAT verbal scores than did their immigrant classmates, many of whom had only been speaking English for a few years.

What many of the American kids I taught did not have was the motivation, self-discipline or work ethic of the foreign-born kids.

Politicians and education bureaucrats can talk all they want about reform, but until the work ethic of U.S. students changes, until they are willing to put in the time and effort to master their subjects, little will change.

A study released in December [2005] by University of Pennsylvania researchers Angela Duckworth and Martin Seligman suggests that the reason so many U.S. students are "falling short of their intellectual potential" is not "inadequate teachers, boring textbooks and large class sizes" and the rest of the usual litany cited by the so-called reformers—but "their failure to exercise self-discipline."

The sad fact is that in the USA, hard work on the part of students is no longer seen as a key factor in academic success.

The groundbreaking work of Harold Stevenson and a multi-national team at the University of Michigan comparing attitudes of Asian and American students sounded the alarm more than a decade ago.

Asian vs. U.S. Students

When asked to identify the most important factors in their performance in math, the percentage of Japanese and Taiwanese students who answered "studying hard" was twice that of American students.

American students named native intelligence, and some said the home environment. But a clear majority of U.S. students put the responsibility on their teachers. A good teacher, they said, was the determining factor in how well they did in math.

"Kids have convinced parents that it is the teacher or the system that is the problem, not their own lack of effort," says Dave Roscher, a chemistry teacher at T.C. Williams in this Washington suburb. "In my day, parents didn't listen when kids complained about teachers. We are supposed to miraculously make kids learn even though they are not working."

As my colleague Ed Cannon puts it: "Today, the teacher is supposed to be responsible for motivating the kid. If they don't learn it is supposed to be our problem, not theirs."

And, of course, busy parents guilt-ridden over the little time they spend with their kids are big subscribers to this theory.

Maybe every generation of kids has wanted to take it easy, but until the past few decades students were not allowed to get away with it. "Nowadays, it's the kids who have the power. When they don't do the work and get lower grades, they scream and yell. Parents side with the kids who pressure teachers to lower standards," says Joel Kaplan, another chemistry teacher at T.C. Williams.

Adolescent Life Is a Vacation

It's that time of year. . . .

Our massive public education bureaucracy lumbers into gear and we are treated once again to annual laments about how overwhelming life is for our adolescent population.

The population that, by the way, is just coming off a vacation of a couple of months and will enjoy another four weeks of vacation during the coming 10 months while the rest of us worker bees, who pay the taxes that fund their 180-day "work" year, . . . are lucky to grab two or three weeks for the entire year.

Taylor Armerding,
North Andover (MA) Eagle-Tribune,
September 10, 2006.

Every year, I have had parents come in to argue about the grades I have given in my AP [Advanced Placement] English classes. To me, my grades are far too generous; to middle-class parents, they are often an affront to their sense of entitlement. If their kids do a modicum of work, many parents expect them to get at least a B. When I have given C's or D's to bright middle-class kids who have done poor or mediocre work, some parents have accused me of destroying their children's futures.

It is not only parents, however, who are siding with students in their attempts to get out of hard work.

Blame Schools, Too

"Schools play into it," says psychiatrist Lawrence Brain, who counsels affluent teenagers throughout the Washington metropolitan area. "I've been amazed to see how easy it is for kids in public schools to manipulate guidance counselors to get them out of classes they don't like. They have been sent a message that they don't have to struggle to achieve if things are not perfect."

Neither the high-stakes state exams, such as Virginia's Standards of Learning, nor the requirements of the No Child Left Behind Act have succeeded in changing that message; both have turned into minimum-competency requirements aimed at the lowest in our school.

Colleges keep complaining that students are coming to them unprepared. Instead of raising admissions standards, however, they keep accepting mediocre students lest cuts have to be made in faculty and administration.

As a teacher, I don't object to the heightened standards required of educators in the No Child Left Behind law. Who among us would say we couldn't do a little better? Nonetheless, teachers have no control over student motivation and ambition, which have to come from the home—and from within each student.

Perhaps the best lesson I can pass along to my upper- and middle-class students is to merely point them in the direction of their foreign-born classmates, who can remind us all that education in America is still more a privilege than a right.

Periodical Bibliography

The following articles have been selected to supplement the diverse views presented in this chapter.

Taylor Armerding
"Pampered Teens Need to Go to Bed Earlier," *North Andover (MA) Eagle-Tribune*, September 10, 2006.

John Cloud
"The Overscheduled Child Myth," *Time*, January 19, 2007.

Katie Couric
"The 411: Teens & Sex," *NBC News*, January 26, 2005.

Janice Shaw Crouse
"Young Teen Sex: Hottest New Pop Culture Concern," Concerned Women for America, January 28, 2005. www.cwfa.org.

Caitlin Flanagan
"Are You There God? It's Me, Monica," *Atlantic Monthly*, January–February 2006.

Catherine Gewertz
"Student Pressure Subject of Debate," *Education Week*, September 13, 2006.

Kevin Johnson
"Cities Grapple with Crime by Kids," *USA Today*, July 12, 2006.

Junior Achievement
"Survey: Teens Feel Intense Pressure to Succeed—Even If It Means Cutting Ethical Corners," December 6, 2006. www.ja.org.

Michael D. Lemonick
"A Teen Twist on Sex," *Time*, September 19, 2005.

Office of Juvenile Justice and Delinquency Prevention
Juvenile Arrests 2004, December 2006.

Kate Raynes-Goldie
"Apathy and Irony," GlobeandMail.com, August 9, 2004. www.theglobeandmail.com.

Alexandra Starr
"They're Not Stupid—They're Lazy," *Slate*, August 8, 2005.

 OPPOSING VIEWPOINTS® SERIES

What Risks Do Youths Face?

Chapter Preface

In the 1980s, news agencies started broadcasting horrific accounts of child abuse and torture committed by Satanic cults. Young children produced stories of heinous acts they had witnessed or been forced to perform, and adults came forward with shocking memories of Satanic abuse that their psyches had supposedly repressed for years. In most of the stories, the abusers were parents who secretly practiced Satanism and used their children in rituals. Soon, according to the *Christian Research Journal*, alleged victims had accused "famous televangelists, police chiefs, FBI agents, the Pope, CIA leaders, U.N. [United Nations] members, millionaires, philanthropists, pastors, teachers, school principals, psychiatrists, and others" of Satanic abuse. Ostensibly, the abusers belonged to cults that engaged in such activities as kidnapping, rape, incest, cannibalism, and forcibly impregnating young girls in order to sacrifice their fetuses. When journalists, police officers, and mental health professionals gave credence to the accounts, the problem of Satanic ritual abuse became all the more legitimate. In response, social workers took dozens of children into protection from their allegedly abusive parents, and some parents were sentenced to many years in prison.

Despite claims that Satanic abuse was widespread, a federally funded study of twelve thousand cases of alleged child abuse found no evidence of such abuse. Similarly, a 1992 report by Kenneth V. Lanning of the FBI insisted, "We now have hundreds of victims alleging that thousands of offenders are abusing and even murdering tens of thousands of people as part of organized Satanic cults, and there is little or no corroborative evidence." Eventually, the parents' convictions were overturned and they were released from prison. Much of the panic, it turns out, was unwarranted.

One explanation for the wild stories is that as people got caught up in the hysteria, they started to truly believe they had memories of victimization that never occurred. In addition, some children's accounts were misunderstood or blown out of proportion by social workers who were trying to protect them. And of course, no one wanted to dismiss horrible accounts that might possibly be based on truth. Dolan Cummings contends in the online publication *spiked*, "It seems incredible now that such charges could ever have been taken seriously, but once the theory had taken hold, it became a point of principle that . . . children must be believed no matter what." The False Memory Syndrome Foundation expands on this:

> How could so many otherwise sensible people have overlooked the impossibility of most of the accusations against parents? Memories . . . of Satanic ritual abuse, memories for which there was never any evidence. Equally disturbing was the fact that the demographic information about accusers and accused did not match what is known about real abuse. [There were] people who remained under arrest for years for putting children in ovens, keeping children in cages and other bizarre acts—none of which had any corroboration.

The hysteria over Satanism was a moral panic that gained strength quickly because it involved young people. Whenever children may be in danger, people tend to want to shield them at all costs. Yet as this case illustrates, mass hysteria can result over some perceived danger to young people, drawing resources away from the real risks they face. "In public discussion of today's youth problems, balance and context has vanished," announces Kirk A. Astroth in *Journal of Extension*. The authors in the next chapter grapple over the dangers young people face and the seriousness of such dangers, debating whether the risks are valid or part of a society-wide panic.

> "Unfortunately, children are now dying
> at the hands of their Internet child mo-
> lesters."

Online Sex Predators Are a Serious Threat to Children

Parry Aftab

Parry Aftab is an Internet privacy lawyer who serves as executive director of Wiredsafety.org., the world's largest cybersafety help group. Her personal Web site is at http://aftab.com. In the viewpoint that follows, she emphasizes that sex predators can solicit any young person online—even those whom adults consider "good" kids who are not at risk. Aftab relays the story of thirteen-year-old Christina Long, the first known murder victim of an Internet sex predator in the United States. In Aftab's assertion, Long's aunt monitored her Internet activity, but still the girl—and many after her—fell prey to an online attacker. This viewpoint was written to encourage parents to ensure children's online safety.

As you read, consider the following questions:

1. How many American teens meet strangers through the Internet, in Aftab's view?

2. What does the author say is significant about Christina Long as a victim?

3. What steps did Long's aunt take to protect her safety online, according to Aftab?

One in four US teen girls reported [in a 2001 survey in *Family PC Magazine*] that they met strangers off the Internet. One in seven boys admitted they did as well. While most of these "Internet friends" turn out to be another teen or preteen, that's not always the case. Unfortunately, children are now dying at the hands of their Internet child molesters, and not all sexual exploitation of children occurs offline.

Christina Long, a thirteen year old honors student and cheerleader, is your child, if you're lucky. This isn't one of "those kind of kids" stories. This story proves that no family is exempt from danger—all children are at risk. This is a call to arms for parents everywhere. We can no longer say "not my kid." Christina Long is our kid. She had a troubled family life earlier, but was in a loving and caring home. Wake up! As an FBI officer once told me, "Go home and hug your children tonight, tell them you love them. Because if you don't someone in there [pointing at the computer] will." Amen.

A Different Kind of Case

The [May] 2002 murder of a suburban Connecticut thirteen-year-old girl has caused many of us serious concern. We hear about online sexual predators and thousands of arrests of people who had previously been trusted in their community. But this case was different. This girl was murdered. Christina Long is the first confirmed death in the U.S. by an Internet sexual predator. Since then, unfortunately, there have been more.

What is also significant about Christina's case was that she wasn't a loner, quiet child. She didn't fit the mold of our perceived victim profile. She was a good student and co-captain

Profile of an Internet Predator

A 35-year-old man anxiously watches the clock on his office wall in anticipation of ending his workday. His coworkers would describe him as a person who tends to isolate himself from others. He really doesn't have a friend, just acquaintances, and these relationships are shallow at best. He has withdrawn over the years from his extended family and often turns down social invitations. He spends considerable time alone. He leaves work as soon as the clock strikes four. Without any delays he heads straight home. If waylaid in any manner he experiences anxiety. He has a compulsion to follow through with his daily routine of leaving work at the same time and going straight home to his computer. He arrives home and doesn't even take his coat off before turning on his computer. After a few keystrokes he has his modem logging on to the Internet. Around his computer is evidence of his long hours in front of the monitor. The last microwave meals he has eaten are stacked nearby. The rest of the apartment appears unlived in. The computer, which he has set up in his bedroom, is the central feature of the residence. He double clicks on a special icon he has set up as a shortcut to his favorite chat system. He selects one of his many fictional characters, deciding on this day to be a 14-year-old boy, "Donny14". He enters a chat room called "£littleboysex" and joins a cyber community of persons of similar interests. The hunt begins.

James F. McLaughlin, "Technophilia: A Modern Day Paraphilia,"
www.ci.keene.nh.us/police/technophilia.html.

of her Catholic School cheerleaders during the day, and at night someone who met at least one stranger from the Internet—the man who killed her. As we understand it, Christina led a double life online. According to reports, she had a Web site that warned those who saw it about her desire to engage in risky behavior. The Web site purportedly boasted that she was ready for anything. Had her father or her aunt (with whom she resided) or others in authority known about what the Web site said, perhaps the situation would have worked out differently. But we will never know.

You should know before we begin, however, that this case was atypical as far as teens meeting sexual predators offline was concerned. At least what we know at that time. Christina's death changed that. This girl was active in school activities, as a cheerleader, and was reported to have many friends. Most child victims are loners. She was also not lured in the typical way by someone seeking to molest her.

She appears to have sought out sexual partners from people she met online.

Christina Long had a troubled family-life. Her mother had left her, and her father gave up residential custody to the mother's sister. The aunt loved Chrissy dearly and the two were devoted to each other. From the time she took custody of Christina, the relationship appears to be ideal for helping Christina avoid online predators. So what went wrong?

Watchful Guardian

The facts are still unclear. Christina's aunt, Shelley (who called her "Chrissy"), told me that she knew about online risks and regularly talked about them with Chrissy. She asked Chrissy to change her screen name, which her aunt thought might be provocative. Chrissy apparently complied. Shelley asked to see Chrissy's Web site, and asked Chrissy to make some changes at the site, to be less suggestive. Chrissy once again appeared to comply. Shelley was very close with her niece. She would drive her to the Mall on a Friday evening and drop her off for a few hours. It was apparently while Chrissy was supposed to be at the Mall that she met the murderer and perhaps others as well. Shelley was watchful and had a good relationship with her niece. But even loving family members can't be everywhere or spot the teen lies so frequently offered, and believed.

This case perplexes me more than any other I have seen. Obviously, given what we have heard about the Web site, Chrissy changed it since her aunt had seen it last. But, what her aunt tells me leads me to believe that this case may be more about a teenager acting out online and getting her bluff called. Since Christina's death we have seen many similar cases, where young teens seek out sexual conversations and suggestive behavior online. It's not real to them, nor can it be. We need to remember that they are only 13 years old. With raging hormones and being bombarded with adult media and sexually explicit materials and communications online, it's remarkable that they can rub two brain cells together. I hope to hold a summit of the leaders in online safety for children to come up with solutions and help for you, as parents. In the meantime, the best advice we have is what we have learned the hard way. Kids have more technology skills than judgment. What sounded good at the time may not be. And the "soul mate" they think they met online may not be a cute 14 year old boy. He may not be cute, 14 or even a boy at all. All children are at risk. Every 13 year old is a potential victim. Even yours.

Hindsight Is 20/20

[There are] special circumstances of this case [and things that] could have been done to help avoid this horrible tragedy. But remember as we examine the telltale signs, before you judge or blame anyone involved in this case—hindsight is 20/20. Instead of looking for someone to blame, we need to extend our prayers and well wishes to the family, and learn from this case. We also need to remember that "there but for the grace of God go all of us." This could have happened to any of our families. And we need to use this time to talk with our children to prevent their following in these tragic footsteps. If others can be saved from this horrible tragedy, this young girl would not have died in vain.

> "While the abduction, rape, and killing
> of children by strangers is very, very
> rare, such incidents receive a lot of me-
> dia coverage."

The Threat of Online Sex Predators Is Exaggerated

Benjamin Radford

Benjamin Radford argues in the following viewpoint that the news media sensationalize stories of children who are assaulted by Internet predators, cases which he says are extremely rare. Radford questions widely publicized statistics that one in five youth receive unwanted solicitations for sex online. The solicitations, he explains, do not lead to sexual encounters and often come from other teens, not adults. The danger that sex offenders pose to children is exaggerated by the media, he claims, and the fact that society is already in a panic over sex predators fuels this alarmism. Radford is managing editor of the critical thinking magazine Skeptical Inquirer.

As you read, consider the following questions:

1. According to Radford, what explanations are likely when a child is missing?

Benjamin Radford, "Predator Panic: A Closer Look," *Skeptical Inquirer*, September 2006. Copyright © 2006, Committee for Skeptical Inquiry. Reproduced by permission.

2. What percentage of children does the author say are actually solicited for sex online?
3. In Radford's contention, what is the source of the commonly cited statistic that there are fifty thousand potential predators online?

To many people, sex offenders pose a serious and growing threat—especially on the Internet. Attorney General Alberto Gonzales has made them a top priority this year [2006], launching raids and arrest sweeps. According to Senate Majority Leader Bill Frist, "the danger to teens is high." On the April 18, 2005, *CBS Evening News* broadcast, correspondent Jim Acosta reported that "when a child is missing, chances are good it was a convicted sex offender." (Acosta is incorrect: If a child goes missing, a convicted sex offender is among the least likely explanations, far behind runaways, family abductions, and the child being lost or injured.) On his NBC series "To Catch a Predator," *Dateline* reporter Chris Hansen claimed that "the scope of the problem is immense," and "seems to be getting worse." Hansen claimed that Web predators are "a national epidemic," while Alberto Gonzales stated that there are 50,000 potential child predators online.

Sex offenders are clearly a real threat, and commit horrific crimes. Those who prey on children are dangerous, but how common are they? How great is the danger? After all, there are many dangers in the world—from lightning to Mad Cow Disease, to school shootings—that are genuine but very remote. Let's examine some widely repeated claims about the threat posed by sex offenders.

One in Five?

According to a May 3, 2006, *ABC News* report, "One in five children is now approached by online predators." This alarming statistic is commonly cited in news stories about [the] prevalence of Internet predators, but the factoid is simply wrong. The "one in five statistic" can be traced back to a 2001 Department of Justice study issued by the National Center for Missing and Exploited Children ("The Youth Internet Safety Survey") that asked 1,501 American teens between 10 and 17 about their online experiences. Anyone bothering to actually read the report will find a very different picture. Among the study's conclusions: "Almost one in five (19 percent). . .received an unwanted sexual solicitation in the past year." (A "sexual solicitation" is defined as a "request to engage in sexual activities or sexual talk or give personal sexual information that were unwanted or, whether wanted or not, made by an adult." Using this definition, one teen asking another teen if he or she is a virgin—or got lucky with a recent date—could be considered "sexual solitication.") Not a single one of the reported solicitations led to any actual sexual contact or assault. Furthermore, almost half of the "sexual solicitations" came not from "predators" or adults but from other teens—in many cases the equivalent of teen flirting. When the study examined the type of Internet "solicitation" parents are most concerned about (e.g., someone who asked to meet the teen somewhere, called the teen on the telephone, or sent gifts), the number drops from "one in five" to just 3 percent.

This is a far cry from an epidemic of children being "approached by online predators." As the study noted, "The problem highlighted in this survey is not just adult males trolling for sex. Much of the offending behavior comes from other youth [and] from females." Furthermore, "Most young people seem to know what to do to deflect these sexual 'come ons.'" The reality is far less grave than the ubiquitous "one in five" statistic suggests.

Recidivism Revisited

Much of the concern over sex offenders stems from the perception that if they have committed one sex offense, they are almost certain to commit more. This is the reason given for why sex offenders (instead of, say, murderers or armed robbers) should be monitored and separated from the public once released from prison. While it's true that serial sex offenders (like serial killers) are by definition likely to strike again, the reality is that very few sex offenders commit further sex crimes.

The high recidivism [the criminal's tendency to repeat the crime] rate among sex offenders is repeated so often that it is accepted as truth, but in fact recent [as of 2006] studies show that the recidivism rates for sex offenses is not unusually high. According to a U.S. Bureau of Justice Statistics study ("Recidivism of Sex Offenders Released from Prison in 1994"), just five percent of sex offenders followed for three years after their release from prison in 1994 were arrested for another sex crime. A study released in 2003 by the Bureau of Justice Statistics found that within three years, 3.3 percent of the released child molesters were arrested again for committing another sex crime against a child. Three to five percent is hardly a high repeat offender rate.

In the largest and most comprehensive study ever done of prison recidivism, the Justice Department found that sex offenders were in fact *less* likely to reoffend than other criminals. The 2003 study of nearly 10,000 men convicted of rape, sexual assault, and child molestation found that sex offenders had a re-arrest rate 25 percent lower than for all other criminals. Part of the reason is that serial sex offenders—those who pose the greatest threat—rarely get released from prison, and the ones who do are unlikely to re-offend. If released sex offenders are in fact no more likely to re-offend than murderers or armed robbers, there seems little justification for the public's fear and the monitoring laws targeting them. (Studies also suggest that sex offenders living near schools or playgrounds are no more likely to commit a sex crime than those living elsewhere.)

While the abduction, rape, and killing of children by strangers is very, very rare, such incidents receive a lot of media coverage, leading the public to overestimate how common these cases are.

Why the Hysteria?

There are several reasons for the hysteria and fear surrounding sexual predators. The predator panic is largely fueled by the news media. News stories emphasize the dangers of Internet predators, convicted sex offenders, pedophiles, and child abductions. The *Today Show*, for example, ran a series of misleading and poorly designed hidden camera "tests" to see if strangers would help a child being abducted. *Dateline NBC* teamed up with a group called Perverted Justice to lure potential online predators to a house with hidden cameras. The program's ratings were so high that it spawned six follow-up "To Catch a Predator" specials. While the many men captured on film supposedly showing up to meet teens for sex is disturbing, questions have been raised about Perverted Justice's methods and accuracy. (For example, the predators are often found in unmoderated chatrooms frequented by those looking for casual sex—hardly places where most children spend their time.) Nor is it surprising that out of over a hundred million Internet users, a fraction of a percentage might be caught in such a sting.

Because there is little hard data on how widespread the problem of Internet predators is, journalists often resort to sensationalism, cobbling a few anecdotes and interviews together into a trend while glossing over data suggesting that the problem may not be as widespread as they claim. But good journalism requires that personal stories—no matter how emotional and compelling—must be balanced with facts and context. Much of the news coverage about sexual predation is not so much wrong as incomplete, lacking perspective.

Explaining the Hysteria Behind Child Abductions

Child abduction strikes fear into the heart of every parent, even though the incidence of stranger child abduction is very rare in America. During the 1980s, people with good intentions publicized vastly inflated figures concerning child abductions. Edwin Sutherland, the famous criminologist, once wrote: "The hysteria produced by child murders is due in part to the fact that the ordinary citizen cannot understand a sex attack on a child . . . Fear is greater because the behavior is so incomprehensible."

Mark Gado, Pedophiles and Child Molesters:
The Slaughter of Innocence, *2004. www.crimelibrary.com.*

Moral Panics

The news media's tendency toward alarmism only partly explains the concern. America is in the grip of a moral panic over sexual predators, and has been for many months. A *moral panic* is a sociological term describing a social reaction to a false or exaggerated threat to social values by moral deviants.

In a discussion of moral panics, sociologist Robert Bartholomew points out that a defining characteristic of the panics is that the "concern about the threat posed by moral deviants and their numerical abundance is far greater than can be objectively verified, despite unsubstantiated claims to the contrary." Furthermore, according to Goode and Ben-Yehuda, during a moral panic "most of the figures cited by moral panic 'claims-makers' are wildly exaggerated."

Indeed, we see exactly this trend in the panic over sexual predators. News stories invariably exaggerate the true extent of sexual predation on the Internet; the magnitude of the danger to children, and the likelihood that sexual predators will strike.

(As it turns out, Attorney General Gonzales had taken his 50,000 Web predator statistic not from any government study or report, but from NBC's *Dateline* TV show. *Dateline*, in turn, had broadcast the number several times without checking its accuracy. In an interview on NPR's *On the Media* program, Hansen admitted that he had no source for the statistic, and stated that "It was attributed to, you know, law enforcement, as an estimate, and it was talked about as sort of an extrapolated number.") According to *Wall Street Journal* writer Carl Bialik, journalists "often will use dubious numbers to advance that goal [of protecting children] . . . one of the reasons that this is allowed to happen is that there isn't really a natural critic. . . . Nobody really wants to go on the record saying, 'It turns out this really isn't a big problem.'"

Panicky Laws

Besides needlessly scaring children and the public, there is a danger to this quasi-fabricated, scare-of-the-week reportage: misleading news stories influence lawmakers, who in turn react with genuine (and voter-friendly) moral outrage. Because nearly any measure intended (or claimed) to protect children will be popular and largely unopposed, politicians trip over themselves in the rush to endorse new laws that "protect the children."

Politicians, child advocates, and journalists denounce current sex offender laws as ineffective and flawed, yet are rarely able to articulate exactly why new laws are needed. Instead, they cite each news story about a kidnapped child or Web predator as proof that more laws are needed, as if sex crimes would cease if only the penalties were harsher, or enough people were monitored. Yet the fact that rare crimes continue to be committed does not necessarily imply that current laws against those crimes are inadequate. By that standard, any law is ineffective if someone violates that law. We don't assume that existing laws against murder are ineffective simply because murders continue to be committed. . . .

[One] high-profile government effort to prevent Internet predation occurred in December 2002, when President Bush signed the Dot-Kids Implementation and Efficiency Act into law, creating a special safe Internet "neighborhood" for children. Elliot Noss, president of Internet address registrar Tucows Inc., correctly predicted that the domain had "absolutely zero" chance of being effective. The ".kids.us" domain is now a largely ignored Internet footnote that has done little or nothing to protect children.

Tragic Misdirection

The issue is not whether children need to be protected; of course they do. The issues are whether the danger to them is great, and whether the measures proposed will ensure their safety. While some efforts—such as longer sentences for repeat offenders—are well-reasoned and likely to be effective, those focused on separating sex offenders from the public are of little value because they are based on a faulty premise. Simply knowing where a released sex offender lives—or is at any given moment—does not ensure that he or she won't be near potential victims. Since relatively few sexual assaults are committed by released sex offenders, the concern over the danger is wildly disproportionate to the real threat. Efforts to protect children are well-intentioned, but legislation should be based on facts and reasoned argument instead of fear in the midst of a national moral panic.

▌ *"Will our children ever be safe?"*

School Violence Is on the Rise

Betsy L. Angert

In the viewpoint that follows, Betsy L. Angert denounces what she sees as an increasing trend toward violence in schools. Despite various countermeasures that have been implemented, shootings continue to plague the nation's schools, she contends. In her opinion, efforts have been misguided, focusing on technology and mandates to prevent violence rather than addressing the offenders themselves. The solution to school violence, she posits, is as complex as the problem itself and must address its many psychological and societal causes. Angert is an educator and author of the Be-Think blog, in which she aims to stimulate thought and emotion.

As you read, consider the following questions:

1. In the author's opinion, what were the details surrounding Brenda Spencer's story?

2. How does Angert describe the Amish schoolhouse killings?

3. What factors contribute to terrorism, according to a source cited by Angert?

Betsy L. Angert, "School Shooting Safeguards. Arm Educators?" Be-Think, October 8, 2006. Reproduced by permission of the author.

In the last few weeks [in the fall of 2006], school shootings have dominated the news. The frequency of these seems to be increasing. People throughout the nation are panicking; what are we to do? President [George W.] Bush spoke of this situation in his Saturday, October 7, 2006, radio address. He proclaimed, "We will bring together teachers, parents, students, administrators, law enforcement officials, and other experts to discuss the best ways to keep violence out of our schools." Conferences have been called. The problem has been discussed for years.

President [Bill] Clinton convened such a forum in 1999. Educators, policy-makers, law enforcement officials, and adolescent-development specialists came to the Radcliffe Institute for Advanced Study on May 21, 2002. Each group was equally intent on investigating the causes and effects of Lethal School Violence. In the symposiums, experts sought solutions. Everyone wanted [and wants] to protect our progeny.

At the time, programs were initiated; yet, the violence continued. In the last month or more, we as a nation are wondering; is there no end? Will our children ever be safe?. . .

Unrelated to Gangs

We know that communities have long been concerned with gang violence. However, what has occurred in recent years differs. On January 29, 1979, individual outbursts came into our collective consciousness. [According to the *Indianapolis Star*,] "Brenda Spencer, 16, opened fire with a .22-caliber rifle at an elementary school across the street from her San Diego, California, home. She killed two people and wounded seven because she 'didn't like Mondays.'"

Upon hearing this story, our country held its breath as it does now. Jointly we release a communal sigh. Still the violence increases as is evident in these last five weeks. There is talk. What measures can we take to guard against weaponry?

[According to cnn.com,] metal detectors were introduced in educational institutions after a 1992 shooting:

> In 1994, the federal government began requiring school safety programs in an attempt to crack down on violence on school grounds. Many schools introduced metal detectors to check for guns, knives and other weapons ... although the Supreme Court eventually overturned the federal requirements, most school safety measures remained in place. In Los Angeles [CA], for instance, [as of 1997] all high schools still use some sort of metal detectors.

However, it is clear, these actions do not secure the premises. Zero tolerance campaigns were invoked. Violations are and were numerous.

Parents, administrators, teachers, and staff were told to observe student behaviors; they were asked to attend to warning signs. Discipline problems were considered predictors; yet, this was not always the case. Offenders did not only come from within the school system, they enter and exist throughout society. Witness the killings within the last month or more [before and during September 2006].

Machines and Mandates

Whatever we choose to reflect upon, when looking at violence in our schools, our homes, or in our airports I ask us to bear in mind that traditional methods for preventing violence are not working. I think we must look at why people do what they do.

Violent crime continues to be a major problem and I suspect this will continue as long as we look for simple solutions. I observe, when we as a country focus on machines and mandates as a means for deterring violence in schools and within society at-large, we ignore the violator. I believe the life of the perpetrator is most telling. This is the key component in a crime that can be influenced and altered. If we address it early enough and treat root causes sincerely and seriously we can make a difference.

However, instead, we look at guns, knives, box cutters, gels, powders, matches, lighters, and bombs as though these are the killers. We work tirelessly to prevent these from entering the systems, schools, airports, office building, and prisons. Rarely do we address the authentic reason for killings. People and what goes on in their heads, hearts, and souls cause death.

I propose we look at life, at our daily existence and the stress our culture promotes, rather than hypothesize how might we use technology and authority to control the minds and misdeeds of men and women. I theorize if we assess the way in which we live and the life standards we choose to accept, then, we might be able to prevent these carnages.

I request that you, dear reader, consider what passes for the "common wisdom." Is it sensible? Please ponder accepted theories and simple solutions with me. Then ask yourself, what might we do to truly change what comes?

More Killings

On Monday, October 2, 2006, a deeply distressed man entered a one-room Amish schoolhouse. He excused all the male pupils and personnel. He was interested in only the young female students. It is not known whether the church-going milkman intended to molest the girls, though there is evidence to suggest that he did. However, what is certain is that the perpetrator shot these little lovelies before taking his own life. Pennsylvania schoolhouse killer Charles Carl Roberts IV revealed in a telephone call to his wife, at the age of twelve he molested two young relatives. Events of 20 years past haunted the man throughout his life. Guilt took Roberts' life and the lives of several young innocent Amish girls.

Five days earlier, in Bailey, Colorado, an armed drifter walked into Platte Canyon High School. He then entered a classroom. The transient demanded that all the men leave the

U.S. School Shooting Incidents Since 2005

March 21, 2005 Red Lake, Minn.	Jeff Weise, 16, killed grandfather and companion, then arrived at school where he killed a teacher, a security guard, 5 students, and finally himself, leaving a total of 10 dead.
Nov. 8, 2005 Jacksboro, Tenn.	One 15-year-old shot and killed an assistant principal at Campbell County High School and seriously wounded two other administrators.
Aug. 24, 2006 Essex, Vt.	Christopher Williams, 27, looking for his ex-girlfriend at Essex Elementary School, shot two teachers, killing one and wounding another. Before going to the school, he had killed the ex-girlfriend's mother. ...
Sept. 29, 2006 Cazenovia, Wis.	A 15-year-old student shot and killed Weston School principal John Klang.
Oct. 3, 2006 Nickel Mines, Pa.	32-year-old Carl Charles Roberts IV entered the one-room West Nickel Mines Amish School and shot 10 schoolgirls, ranging in age from 6 to 13 years old, and then himself. Five of the girls and Roberts died.
Jan. 3, 2007 Tacoma, Wash.	Douglas Chanthabouly, 18, shot fellow student Samnang Kok, 17, in the hallway of Henry Foss High School.
April 16, 2007 Blacksburg, Va.	A 23-year-old Virginia Tech student, Cho Seung-Hui, killed two in a dorm, then killed 30 more 2 hours later in a classroom building. His suicide brought the death toll to 33, making the shooting rampage the most deadly in U.S. history. Fifteen others were wounded.

TAKEN FROM: Infoplease.com, "A Time Line of Recent Worldwide School Shootings," Pearson Education, 2007. www.infoplease.com.

area. He wanted to be alone with the girls he corralled into a classroom. According to a student and her mother, Duane R. Morrison seemed to prefer smaller, blonde girls. This disturbed wanderer with his quarry of petite flaxen hair maidens proceeded to sexually assault some of the six young girls he held hostage. Ultimately, he shot one before killing himself. Some social scientists are theorizing girls are the targets in school violence. [MSNBC reports that] after the crime, at their home in Tulsa, Oklahoma, Morrison's stepmother said she and her husband, Bob Morrison, "have no record of his having any trouble before." "We just know the way he was raised," Billie Morrison said, declining to elaborate.

How was he raised? Some experts think the relationships established in the lives of the killers might offer answers. In the series of recent rampages there is a seemingly notable consistency. [According to the *Christian Science Monitor*,]

> "The predominant pattern in school shootings of the past three decades is that girls are the victims," says Katherine Newman, a Princeton University sociologist whose recent book examines the roots of "rampage" shootings in rural schools.
>
> Dr. Newman has researched 21 school shootings since the 1970s. Though it's impossible to know whether girls were randomly victimized in those cases, she says, "in every case in the US since the early 1970s we do note this pattern" of girls being the majority of victims.

A Complex Problem

Prior to these two incidents, the focus and fantasy was on troubled adolescents. These were thought to be the persons responsible for such horrendous school crimes. Some behavior experts hypothesized: violent young persons had been bullied in school. They were browbeaten at home. These youthful aggressors were tormented by their own inner struggles. They act out after years of deep-seated frustration. . . .

I believe the more recent incidents confirm the quandary has many causes. The dilemma is not limited to youth acting out against their harassing, haranguing, or hounding classmates. These incidents are not only a reaction to discrimination from peers. Parents are not the central problem. This transgression is, as all others, complex.

The complexities that cause violent crime in our nation's schools are similar to those that create terrorism. [A report by Rex A. Hudson explains,]

> Terrorism usually results from multiple causal factors—not only psychological but also economic, political, religious, and sociological factors, among others. There is even a hypothesis that it is caused by physiological factors, as discussed below. Because terrorism is a multi-causal phenomenon, it would be simplistic and erroneous to explain an act of terrorism by a single cause, such as the psychological need of the terrorist to perpetrate an act of violence.

> For Paul Wilkinson (1977), the causes of revolution and political violence in general are also the causes of terrorism. These include ethnic conflicts, religious and ideological conflicts, poverty, modernization stresses, political inequities, lack of peaceful communications channels, traditions of violence, the existence of a revolutionary group, governmental weakness and ineptness, erosions of confidence in a regime, and deep divisions within governing elites and leadership groups.

International terrorists, sadistic student rebels, and lone executors have a common bond; society and stressors impact their lives severely.

Students' killers are often exposed to frequent slights from peers or parents, just as some terrorists feel slighted by our treatment of their culture and religious practices. These snubs are evident if society as a whole and those functioning within the system choose to recognize them. The stress in young lives can be reduced or eliminated if we attend to these grievances quickly.

Frustration and Persecution

We might realize that lone shooters, those that walk into our schools, also are victims of a fragile upbringing. There are reasons that. these solitary shooters might aim at young girls, blondes, or the most innocent among us. Again, if we as a community choose to be aware of what we are creating for our children, we can save them before they become adult or adolescent killers.

Religious or political zealots, the defiant, defensive, and the righteous also are products of their environment. They may act out against nations or peoples; still, the source of their rage is apparent if we choose to look for it. Each of these executors feels persecuted and why not.

In a world where frustrations are ignored or attributed to authority figures, women, or circumstances beyond our control, there is much to feel frustrated about. Students feel stuck in school, at home, or in lives that demand much of them and give little in return. Adults, loners and cult followers alike, feel lost in the unresolved circumstances of their past and present. They want to affect the future. However, in the future, as in the present, and the past, people are not the focus. Folly and failed systems are.

We evaluate preventive mechanized and legal measures. We disregard the fact that these are not effective.

I propose we look at life, at our daily existence and the stresses our cultures promote. I theorize if we assess the way in which we live, the life standards we accept, then, we might be able to prevent these mass and individual tragedies.

"Weapon carrying on school property declined significantly, from 11.8% in 1993 to 6.1% in 2003."

School Violence Is Decreasing

Centers for Disease Control and Prevention

In the next viewpoint, the Centers for Disease Control and Prevention (CDC) analyzes the results of its national Youth Risk Behavior Survey and surmises that school violence has declined since 1991. In evaluating the data, CDC discovered that high school students engage in fewer physical fights at school and are less likely to carry weapons on school grounds, while the number of teens injured with a weapon at school has remained constant. However, the organization emphasizes that schools and communities must continue to work toward preventing violence and increasing safety in schools. CDC is the government agency that works to improve the health of all Americans.

As you read, consider the following questions:

1. Name two of the national health objectives for 2010, according to the CDC.
2. What four school-related adolescent behaviors were assessed in the study?

Centers for Disease Control and Prevention, "Violence-Related Behaviors Among High School Students—United States, 1991–2003," *Morbidity and Mortality Weekly Report*, vol. 53, July 30, 2004, pp. 651–53.

3. According to the CDC, which youth behavior increased from 1993 to 2003?

Homicide and suicide are responsible for approximately one-fourth of deaths among persons aged 10–24 years in the United States [according to *National Vital Statistics Reports*, 2003]. Two of the national health objectives [set by Department of Health and Human Services] for 2010 are to reduce the prevalence of physical fighting among adolescents to ≤32% and to reduce the prevalence of carrying a weapon by adolescents on school property to ≤4.9%. To examine changes in violence-related behaviors among high school students in the United-States during 1991–2003, CDC [Centers for Disease Control and Prevention] analyzed data from the national Youth Risk Behavior Survey (YRBS). This report summarizes the results of that analysis, which indicated that most violence-related behaviors decreased during 1991–2003; however, students increasingly were likely to miss school because they felt too unsafe to attend. In addition, in 2003, nearly one in 10 high school students reported being threatened or injured with a weapon on school property during the preceding 12 months. Schools and communities should continue efforts to establish physical and social environments that prevent violence and promote actual and perceived safety in schools.

The Sampling Process

The national YRBS, a component of CDC's Youth Risk Behavior Surveillance System, used independent three-stage (i.e., primary sampling units, schools, and classes) cluster samples for the 1991–2003 surveys to obtain cross-sectional data representative of public- and private-school students in grades 9–12 in the 50 states and the District of Columbia. During 1991–2003, sample sizes ranged from 10,904 to 16,296, school response rates ranged from 70% to 81%, student response rates ranged from 83% to 90%, and overall response rates ranged from 60% to 70%. For each cross-sectional national survey, students completed an anonymous, self-administered questionnaire that included identically worded questions about violence.

For this analysis, temporal changes during 1991–2003 for three behaviors were assessed: 1) weapon (e.g., a gun, knife, or club) carrying (on ≤1 of the 30 days preceding the survey), 2) physical fighting (one or more times during the 12 months preceding the survey), and 3) being in a physical fight that resulted in injuries that had to be treated by a doctor or nurse (one or more times during the 12 months preceding the survey). In addition, temporal changes from 1993–2003 for four school-related behaviors were assessed: 1) weapon carrying on school property (on ≤1 of the 30 days preceding the survey), 2) physical fighting on school property (one or more times during the 12 months preceding the survey), 3) being threatened or injured with a weapon on school property (one or more times during the 12 months preceding the survey), and 4) not going to school because of safety concerns (i.e., feeling too unsafe at school or on the way to or from school on ≤1 of the 30 days preceding the survey). Data are presented only for non-Hispanic black, non-Hispanic white, and Hispanic students because the numbers of students from other racial/ethnic populations were too small for meaningful analysis. . . .

Study Findings

Significant and quadratic trends were detected for weapon carrying. Overall, the prevalence of weapon carrying declined significantly, from 26.1% in 1991 to 18.3% in 1997, and then leveled off through 2003 (17.1%). Similar significant linear and quadratic trends were detected among female, male, white, 10th-, 11th-, and 12th-grade students. Among black, Hispanic, and 9th-grade students, a significant linear decline was detected during 1991–2003.

Percentage of High School Students Who Brought a Weapon to School

	1993 %	1995 %	1997 %	1999 %	2001 %	2003 %
Overall	**11.8**	**9.8**	**8.5**	**6.9**	**6.4**	**6.1**
Sex						
Female	5.1	4.9	3.7	2.8	2.9	3.1
Male	17.9	14.3	12.5	11.0	10.2	8.9
Race/Ethnicity						
White, non-Hispanic	10.9	9.0	7.8	6.4	6.1	5.5
Black, non-Hispanic	15.0	10.3	9.2	5.0	6.3	6.9
Hispanic	13.3	14.1	10.4	7.9	6.4	6.0
Grade						
9th	12.6	10.7	10.2	7.2	6.7	5.3
10th	11.5	10.4	7.7	6.6	6.7	6.0
11th	11.9	10.2	9.4	7.0	6.1	6.6
12th	10.8	7.6	7.0	6.2	6.0	6.4

TAKEN FROM: Centers for Disease Control and Prevention, *Morbidity and Mortality Weekly Report,* July 30, 2004.

Overall, physical fighting declined significantly, from 42.5% in 1991 to 33.0% in 2003. Physical fighting also declined significantly among all subgroups except 11th-grade students. Among 11th-grade students, physical fighting declined during 1991–1999 and then remained level through 2003. No significant changes were detected in the prevalence of being injured in a physical fight overall or by subgroup.

Weapon carrying on school property declined significantly, from 11.8% in 1993 to 6.1% in 2003. Weapon carrying also declined significantly among female, male, white, Hispanic, 9th-, 10th-, and 11th-grade students. Significant linear and quadratic trends were detected for weapon carrying on school property among black and 12th-grade students, with the prevalence of carrying a weapon on school property declining during 1993–1999 and then remaining level through 2003.

Physical fighting on school property declined significantly, from 16.2% in 1993 to 12.8% in 2003. A similar significant linear trend was detected among all subgroups.

No significant changes were detected in the prevalence of being threatened or injured with a weapon on school property during 1993–2003 overall or among female, male, Hispanic, 10th-, and 12th-grade students. A significant linear increase during 1993–2003 was detected among white and 9th-grade students. Among black students, being threatened or injured with a weapon on school properly declined during 1993–1999 and then increased through 2003. Among 11th-grade students, being threatened or injured with a weapon on school property declined during 1993–1999 and then remained level through 2003.

Not going to school because of safety concerns increased significantly, from 4.4% in 1993 to 5.4% in 2003. Not going to school because of safety concerns also increased significantly among female, white, and 11th-grade students. No significant changes were detected during 1993–2003 among male, black, Hispanic, 9th-, 10th-, and 12th-grade students.

> *"Gay teens are two to three times more
> likely to attempt suicide than their het-
> erosexual peers."*

Gay Teen Suicide Is Common

Letitia L. Star

*In the viewpoint that follows, Letitia L. Star maintains that ho-
mosexual youths attempt suicide at a much higher rate than
heterosexual youths do. She attributes this in part to the bullying, depression, and anxiety experienced by many gay teens because of their sexuality. In response to these problems, a suicide
prevention hotline especially for young gays has been established
and, Star states, has fielded thousands of calls from youths in
crisis. As a freelance writer, Star often reports on youth and
families. This viewpoint was published on the Web site Connect
for Kids, which disseminates information on children and families.*

As you read, consider the following questions:

1. According to statistics provided by Star, what percentage
   of teens report that youths who are or may be gay are
   teased or bullied?
2. What are the suicide risk factors that Jorge Valencia
   claims are specific to gay youth?

Letitia L. Star, "The Trevor Project: Help for Suicidal Gay Teens," *Connect for Kids*,
www.connectforkids.org, April 10, 2006. Reproduced by permission.

3. How many calls has The Trevor Project hotline received, according to the author?

Suicide ranks as the third leading cause of death among young people between the ages of 15 and 29—outranked only by accidents and homicides. And for some teens the risk is even greater—national and state surveys indicate that gay and lesbian teens are far more likely than their heterosexual peers to attempt suicide.

While there are a number of hotlines and other resources for depressed teens in crisis, The Trevor Project stands out for its focus on gay and questioning teens. The project is a non-profit 501-3-c [tax-exempted] headquartered in Beverly Hills, California, and operates the nation's only 24-hour suicide prevention helpline especially geared towards gay and questioning youth.

As part of its mission to aid in suicide prevention and to promote acceptance of gay and questioning teenagers, The Trevor Project also provides other services, including guidance and resources for teens, teachers, parents and educators.

The Trevor Project hotline: 866-4-U-TREVOR (866-488-7386)

Understanding the Risk

Sexual orientation and gender identity issues are not, in and of themselves, risk factors for suicide. However, gay teens are two to three times more likely to attempt suicide than their heterosexual peers, according to the 1989 report, "The Secretary's Task Force on Youth Suicide" by Paul Gibson for the U.S. Dept. of Health & Human Services. That is believed to be partly due to their increased risk of depression and anxiety triggered by the widespread harassment and bullying of gay teens.

According to a national survey released in 2002 by the National Mental Health Association [NMHA], 78% of teens reported that kids who are gay or thought to be gay are teased or bullied in their schools and communities.

"When bullied, gay youth and those thought to be gay face an increased risk for depression, anxiety disorders, school failure and suicide," said Michael Faenza, former president of the NMHA. . . .

A National Issue

The Massachusetts Youth Risk Behavior Survey found that lesbian, gay, bisexual and transgender (LGBT) teens are almost four times more likely to attempt suicide and five times more likely to receive medical treatment for an attempt than heterosexual youth—somewhat higher than the national figures.

There has been controversy over how direct government public health efforts aimed at teen suicide prevention should be about the specific risks to gay and questioning teens. For example, in 2005 two employees of the federal Substance Abuse and Mental Health Services Administration (SAMHSA) asked organizers to remove the words "gay," "lesbian," "bisexual" and "transgender" from the conference of the Suicide Prevention Resource Center.

The specific risks to gay teens are real, say [gay] advocates. "We can pretty much say that this is what's going on throughout the country. The Massachusetts survey has been conducted every two years since 1993 with consistent results. Studies in other cities and states such as Vermont, Chicago [IL] and San Francisco [CA] have had similar findings," said Jorge Valencia, executive director of The Trevor Project.

"These statistics indicate a real need. We believe that these high rates are preventable," he commented. "Suicide risk factors specific to gay youth include lack of family acceptance, being ostracized due to gender non-conformity and feeling fear of loss when coming out," said Valencia. "But even if young people aren't facing a gay-related risk factor, knowing

Tolerance and Understanding Are Key

Some in our population teach and preach that there is something inherently wrong with homosexuality and that homosexuality is a "sin" and an unacceptable and morally wrong "choice." Some in our society, like a recent writer to [*Concord Monitor,*] categorize homosexuality as "abnormal," "disgusting" and "perverted."

My suggestion is that we recognize the potential harm we are inflicting on nearly 10 percent of our youth population by promoting anything but acceptance, tolerance and understanding for each of them. . . .

We must combat views that make our gay youth feel bad about their sexual orientation.

Douglas Dickson,
Concord Monitor Online *(NH), August 27, 2006.*
www.concordmonitor.com.

that they can talk to another gay person about suicide makes them feel additionally comfortable." . . .

How It Began

The helpline was created in 1998 to coincide with the HBO airing of the Academy-Award winning short film "Trevor," an 18-minute drama about a fictional 13-year-old gay teen who makes an unsuccessful suicide attempt when rejected because of his sexuality. The film's creators, Randy Stone, Peggy Rajski, and James Lecesne established the helpline with a generous start-up grant from The Colin Higgins Foundation, which assists organizations in the area of AIDS education and advocacy and empowerment of the GLBT community. [As of April 2006,] the helpline has received over 30,000 calls, and handles a monthly average of 750 to 1,000 calls.

"The majority of calls come in right after school gets out. Gay teens who are harassed, verbally abused and physically assaulted feel very alone," said Valencia. "Knowing that there is someone they can speak with means a lot to them, especially if they are not getting support from family, community, schools or their religion. They need to talk with people who want them to stay alive and offer them the necessary resources."

"Gay and questioning youth don't have to be suicidal to call. We are here for youth in crisis; and that crisis is defined by them, not us. For example, a teen may face a relationship issue and we are here to help them hash it out," commented [Andy] Scheer [of The Trevor Project].

"Not all callers are suicidal, but they need to talk about their feelings. Young people are calling from rural America where there are very few places for outreach," said David Paisley, who is deputy director of San Francisco Suicide Prevention, a Trevor Helpline partner.

Anyone who is concerned that a gay teen may be suicidal is encouraged to call as well. Parents, teachers, educators, friends and loved ones are welcome to phone for feedback, referrals and information.

> "Homosexuals . . . have won great inroads into public schools by claiming that 'gay' teens are killing themselves in record numbers."

The Number of Gay Teen Suicides Is Exaggerated

Traditional Values Coalition

In the viewpoint that follows, Traditional Values Coalition (TVC) contests claims that 30 percent of teens who attempt suicide are homosexual and that gay teens are at a high risk of suicide. These statistics, the coalition alleges, are based on a skewed report provided by gay advocates who wish to further what TVC calls the homosexual agenda. In support of this, the coalition points to recent research that gay teens are no more likely to attempt suicide than straight teens. Moreovoer, TVC asserts, such inflated statistics unfairly pathologize gay youths. Traditional Values Coalition lobbies for churches and focuses on restoring values needed to maintain strong, unified families.

As you read, consider the following questions:

1. In the coalition's opinion, what school programs have been established because of the claim that 30 percent of teens who attempt suicide are gay?

Traditional Values Coalition, "Homosexual Urban Legend: 30% of Teen Suicide Victims Are Homosexuals," *www.traditionalvalues.org.* Reproduced by permission.

2. What are two reasons previous studies on gay teen suicide were flawed, according to Savin-Williams in the viewpoint?

3. On what speculation did Paul Gibson base his statistic that 30 percent of teens who attempt suicide are homosexual, according to TVC?

For more than a decade, Traditional Values Coalition has been repeatedly exposing the myth of an "epidemic" of "homosexual" teen suicides.

Now, a psychologist has published the results of two studies that—once again—expose the Homosexual Urban Legend that teens who have homosexual feelings are committing suicides in record numbers.

Homosexual activists have repeatedly claimed for more than ten years that 30% of all teens who have attempted suicide are homosexuals. The mythological 30% figure was concocted by a homosexual social worker named Paul Gibson who wrote "Gay Male and Lesbian Youth Suicide," published in 1989. It has been thoroughly debunked, but homosexuals continue to use the figure because it supports their political and social agenda.

This 30% myth has been used over and over again to convince public school officials to establish pro-homosexual counseling programs, special clubs for homosexuals run by Gay, Lesbian, and Straight Education Network (GLSEN) teenagers, and sensitivity/anti-homophobia training sessions to convince straight students that homosexual behavior is normal.

Exposing the Myth

The latest studies that expose the 30% urban legend appear in the December 2001 issue of *Journal of Consulting and Clinical Psychology*. The author of these studies is Cornell University psychologist Ritch Savin-Williams.

Savin-Williams says previous homosexual teen suicide studies were flawed and exaggerated because they were drawn from group 'homes or runaway shelters where the most troubled teens gather. Researchers also took at face value the claims that these teens made about their attempts at suicide.

Savin-Williams surveyed a more representative group of teens. He focused on 349 students, ages 17 to 25. When these students told him they had tried to kill themselves, he asked them what method they had used.

Savin-Williams discovered the following:

- Over half of these reported suicide attempts turned out to be "thinking about it" rather than attempting it.

- One study of 83 women showed a true suicide rate of 13% for those who hadn't attended a support group. (Between 7% and 13% of all teens have tried to kill themselves, according to latest figures.)

- Another survey of 266 college men and women found that teens who think they are homosexuals were not much more likely to have attempted suicide than straight students. Homosexual students were more likely to have reported "attempts," but these turned out to be "thinking" about suicide rather than actually doing it.

According to Savin-Williams, homosexual teen suicide statistics unfairly "pathologize gay youth, and that's not fair to them." Savin-Williams is not "anti-homosexual," but has apparently attempted to conduct honest research.

In fact, Beth Reis, a pro-homosexual activist with the Safe Schools Coalition solicited a clarification from Savin-Williams on his research. Reis was concerned that his work might have been misreported in the media. It was not.

Savin-Williams responded to her by noting: "When I solicit a broad spectrum of youths with same sex attractions, and not only those who openly identify as gay, lesbian, or bisexual while in high school, and asked in-depth questions about their suicide history, I found statistically no difference

The Gay Youth Suicide Myth

Voicing concern over suicide risk for "gay youth," homo-sexual activists are pushing pro-homosexual programs in the schools, which will invariably ensnare vulnerable teens who might otherwise have avoided the destructive homo-sexual lifestyle. Their diagnosis: gay youths need affirmation of their homosexuality in a "homophobic" world, or they may become suicidal. The proffered solution: affirmation programs that make gay youths comfortable with being ho-mosexual and the rest of the student population comfort-able with the concept of homosexuality. Once everyone ac-cepts homosexuality as "normal" and "natural," gay youth will achieve high self-esteem and avoid suicidal behavior.

But this view is based on the aims and values of the gay activist movement, not on any solid scientific assessment. For starters, it ignores the possibility that homosexuality is a condition—apart from societal acceptance or nonaccep-tance—that often leads to unhealthy behavior, which leads to unhappiness.

Peter LaBarbera, Insight, *February 1994.*

in the suicide attempt rate based on sexual attractions. Al-though same-sex attracted youths initially reported a higher rate of suicide attempts, on further probing this sexual attrac-tion disappeared." Savin-Williams believes that pro-homosexual adults have done a disservice to homosexual teens by creating a "suffering, suicidal, tragic" script for them that often leads these troubled teens to report attempted suicides when these events did not occur.

According to Savin-Williams, homosexuals do a disservice to "gay" teens when they "paint them with one rather narrow negative brush stroke." Homosexuals, however, have won great inroads into public schools by claiming that "gay" teens are killing themselves in record numbers. This 30% suicide claim is now gone and activists are finally being forced to admit this fact—something they had refused to do for more than a decade.

Perpetuating the Urban Legend

Human Rights Campaign (HRC), an aggressive homosexual group, has continuously pushed the 30% urban legend over the years. HRC spokesman David Smith reluctantly admitted that the 30% figure is wrong, but he told *USA Today*, "Nobody disputes the fact being gay or lesbian in high school is not a very pleasant experience. The core problem is prejudice and harassment that goes unchecked in school settings. School officials take no action. We need to address that problem head-on."

Homosexual activists like David Smith have ignored more than a decade of studies debunking the 30% statistic. As noted above, the 30% urban legend was created by homosexual social worker Paul Gibson in 1989. Gibson's flawed study became an appendix in a Health and Human Services [HHS] report entitled, "Gay Male and Lesbian Youth Suicide." Although Gibson's work was repudiated by then-secretary of HHS, Dr. Louis W. Sullivan, homosexual activists were successful in using Gibson's work to push for "gay" counseling programs and "tolerance" curricula in our nation's public schools. Gibson's report, for example, was used by activists in Massachusetts to establish a state-wide gay and lesbian youth commission funded with millions of dollars by the state.

Gibson's 30% figure was based, in part, on a quotation from a homosexual activist in the *Washington Blade* who speculated that 3,000 homosexual teens killed themselves each year.

Analyzing Gibson's Report

Activists continue to use his report, despite the fact that his work has been debunked. What are the most frequently quoted "facts" from Gibson's report? They are:

1. That homosexual teens account for one third of all teen suicides;

2. That homosexual teens are two to three times more likely to commit suicide than their heterosexual counter-parts;

3. That suicide is the leading cause of death among "gay" and "lesbian" youth;

4. That "gay" youth suicide is caused by internalized homophobia and violence directed against struggling teen homosexuals.

Few journalists took the time to actually analyze Gibson's report when it came out. As a result, his non-facts became part of the culture. One enterprising journalist who actually studied the report is Delia M. Rios with the Newhouse News Service. Her report, "Statistics on gay suicides are baseless, researchers say," was published in the *Seattle Times* on May 22, 1997.

Rios quoted Peter Muehrer, with the National Institutes of Mental Health. Muehrer said most major research studies citing a link between sexual orientation and suicide are "limited in both quantity and quality." He also said there are no agreed-upon standards in suicide research, and reliable methods for measuring suicide attempts are nonexistent.

> Because of these factors, said Muehrer, "it is not possible to accurately compare suicide attempt rates between gay and lesbian youth and non-gay youth in the general population." According to Muehrer, "There is no scientific evidence to support this (30%) figure."

Peter LaBarbera, author of "The Gay Youth Suicide Myth" published by the Family Research Council, quotes Dr. David Shaffer, one of the nation's leading authorities on youth suicide. Shaffer analyzed Gibson's figures and observed: "I struggled for a long time over [Gibson's] mathematics, but, in the end, it seemed more like hocus-pocus than math."

In short, while Gibson's non-facts are still being used by homosexuals to promote the recruitment and seduction of children in our nation's public schools, there is now new evidence from Cornell's Savin-Williams, showing that suicide among homosexual teens is no more likely than among heterosexual teenagers.

"Relative to adults, adolescents are more susceptible to the influence of their peers in risky situations."

Peer Pressure Is a Risk for Adolescents

Margo Gardner and Laurence Steinberg

Margo Gardner and Laurence Steinberg in the Psychology Department of Temple University conducted a study to assess the impact of peer influence on risky decision making. The following viewpoint is excerpted from the study, in which they found that the presence of peers encourages adolescents to take chancier risks than they do when alone. Youths who listened to their peers' advice when playing a risk-taking game, for example, made riskier choices than those who played by themselves, according to the researchers. In their view, the tendency to take risks decreases with age, as does the effect of peer influence on risk taking.

As you read, consider the following questions:

1. What are the study's hypotheses, as set forth by the authors?

Margo Gardner and Laurence Steinberg, "Peer Influence on Risk Taking, Risk Preference, and Risky Decision Making in Adolescence and Adulthood: An Experimental Study," *Developmental Psychology*, vol. 41, no. 4, July 2005, pp. 626–32. Copyright © 2005 by the American Psychological Association. Reproduced by permission.

2. How do Gardner and Steinberg describe the game Chicken?

3. According to the authors, which five hypothetical situations were used to assess participants' risky decision making?

A lthough adolescent risk taking often occurs in groups, it is not known whether the greater prevalence of group risk taking observed among adolescents stems from the fact that adolescents spend more time in peer groups than adults do or from the heightened levels of susceptibility to peer influence that have been shown to characterize adolescence. In other words, it is not clear whether adolescents simply have more opportunities to engage in group risk taking than do adults or whether, when faced with behavioral decisions in a peer group context, adolescents are more easily swayed toward risky choices. . . .

The goal of the present study is therefore to examine whether adolescents, relative to adults, are more likely to take risks when their peers are present.

Hypotheses and Method

In the present study, we examined the differential effects of the presence of peers on risk taking, risk preference, and risky decision making among adolescents ([average] age = 14), youths ([average] age = 19), and adults ([average] age = 37). Our three primary hypotheses were as follows:

Hypothesis 1. Risk taking, risk preference, and risky decision making will decrease with age.

Hypothesis 2. On average, individuals will demonstrate more risk taking, greater risk preference, and more risky decision making when in the company of their peers than when alone.

Hypothesis 3. The difference between levels of risk taking, risk preference, and risky decision making with and without the presence of peers will decrease with age. That is, group effects on risk orientation will be greater among adolescents than among youths, and greater among youths than among adults. .

Our sample included 106 adolescents (54 girls and 52 boys), ages 13 to 16, 105 youths (53 women and 52 men), ages 18 to 22, and 95 adults (48 women and 47 men), ages 24 and older. [The participants were placed into groups of 3 with people of their same age and gender whom they knew prior to the study.]

Groups of 3 were then randomly assigned to a group condition (in which all 3 participants completed the battery of measures at the same time, in the same room, and communicated with each other while completing the tasks and measures) or to a sole participant condition (in which each of the 3 participants completed the battery of measures alone while the other 2 participants waited outside the room where the session took place). . . .

Measures

Risk taking. Risk taking was assessed with a video game called "Chicken." Chicken is played on a laptop computer and requires participants to make decisions about whether to stop a car that is moving across the screen once a traffic light turns from green to yellow. The appearance of the yellow light signals the impending appearance of a red traffic light, as well as a potential crash if the car is still moving when the red light appears. Chicken was selected because it measures risk taking in the moment rather than the more deliberative form of risk taking assessed in many studies, in which participants have unlimited time to consider and evaluate all potential decisions and outcomes. Additionally, Chicken requires participants to make actual decisions in a risky situation, rather than simply requiring participants to report what they would do in a hypothetical risky situation.

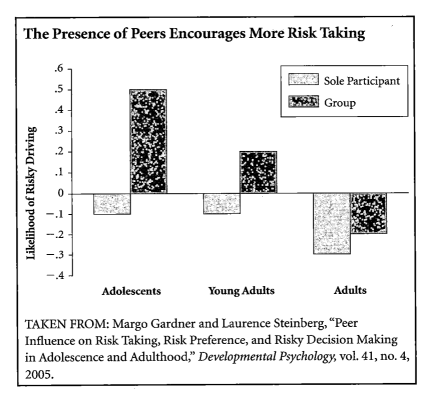

The Presence of Peers Encourages More Risk Taking

TAKEN FROM: Margo Gardner and Laurence Steinberg, "Peer Influence on Risk Taking, Risk Preference, and Risky Decision Making in Adolescence and Adulthood," *Developmental Psychology*, vol. 41, no. 4, 2005.

The game is played from a third-person, side-view perspective and consists of 15 trials. In each trial, participants watched an animated car move across the screen for a predetermined amount of time until a yellow traffic light appeared. Before the first trial players were informed that at some unknown point after the yellow light appeared, the traffic light would turn red and a wall would pop up in front of the car. Players were told that the object of the game was to allow the car to move as far as possible without crashing into the wall. . . .

Participants in the group condition took turns playing the game, but all of them completed 15 trials in a row, as did participants in the sole participant condition. In the group condition, while one participant was playing the game, the other two were told that they could call out advice about whether to allow the car to keep moving or to stop it. The player was instructed that he or she could choose whether to follow the advice of his or her peers.

Risk preference. A shortened, modified version of the Benthin Risk Perception Measure was used to assess risk preference. This measure assesses both risk perception (the extent to which one perceives a given activity as carrying the potential for adverse consequences) and risk preference (whether one believes the benefits inherent in an activity outweigh the costs, or vice versa). . . .

In completing the Risk Preference Scale, participants were presented with five hypothetical scenarios involving risky behavior. These scenarios included having sex without a condom, riding in a car driven by someone who has been drinking, trying a new drug that one does not know anything about, breaking into a store at night and stealing something that one really wants, and driving over 90 mph on the highway at night. They were then asked to rate on a 4-point scale ranging from 1 (*risks are much greater than benefits*) to 4 (*benefits are much greater than risks*) how the risks compared with the benefits of the activity. A mean risk-benefit consideration score was then calculated for each participant by averaging responses across the five scenarios.

Individuals in the sole participant condition read the scenarios from index cards and indicated their choices on a response card displaying the 4-point scale. Group condition participants followed the same procedure but were told that they could discuss each question. However, they were instructed that they need not reach a consensus and that each could make a final decision at any time. Each participant had his or her own set of response cards and had an unobstructed view of the others' response cards. The administrator recorded individuals' responses.

Risky decision making. Risky decision making was assessed via the Youth Decision-Making Questionnaire. Participants were presented with five hypothetical dilemmas, each involving a risky decision. The dilemmas included decisions about allowing friends to bring drugs into one's home, stealing a car, cheating on an exam, shoplifting, and skipping work without an excuse, all of which adolescents, college undergraduates, and adults potentially could have done. . . .

Effects of Peer Presence on Risk Taking

We found significant effects of peer presence on all three measures of risk orientation. Specifically, compared with those who completed the measures by themselves, participants who completed the same measures with peers present took more risks during the risk-taking game, gave greater weight to the benefits rather than the costs of risky activities, and were more likely to select risky courses of action in the risky decision-making situations. . . .

Between adolescence and adulthood there is a significant decline in both risk taking and risky decision making. In addition, our findings suggest that, in some situations, individuals may take more risks, evaluate risky behavior more positively, and make more risky decisions when they are with their peers than when they are by themselves. Most importantly, the effects of peer presence on both risk taking and risky decision making vary as a function of age. That is, although the sample as a whole took more risks and made more risky decisions in groups than when alone, this effect was more pronounced during middle and late adolescence than during adulthood. Thus, relative to adults, adolescents are more susceptible to the influence of their peers in risky situations.

"Peers . . . can push in positive directions as well."

Peer Pressure Is
Not Necessarily a Risk
for Adolescents

Colleen Gengler

*Colleen Gengler argues in the following viewpoint that parents
misunderstand the influence of peer pressure on their children.
Peer pressure, she avers, can be a positive influence. Furthermore, young people's desire to behave badly when they are with
friends comes from within themselves, she asserts. What parents
should remember, she advises, is that parents retain a stronger
influence over their children's morals, beliefs, and future choices
than they think. Gengler, a family relations specialist, works at
the University of Minnesota Extension Service Regional Center
in Worthington, which focuses on positive parenting of kids.*

As you read, consider the following questions:

1. What are some of the ways in which peer pressure is
   misunderstood, in the author's opinion?

Colleen Gengler, "Peer Pressure on Teens Is Often Misunderstood," *University of Minnesota Extension News*, August 24, 2005. Reproduced by permission.

2. In Gengler's view, what should parents do instead of blaming their teen's friends?

3. On what issues are teens influenced by their parents, according to the author?

Parents of teens typically talk about peer pressure a lot. They sometimes blame peer pressure when teens make poor choices. But peer pressure is often misunderstood in a number of ways.

The Truth About Peer Pressure

Peer pressure isn't always negative. Peers may pressure others into negative behaviors or away from positive behaviors, but can push in positive directions as well. One of the best examples is peer pressure not to smoke. According to parenting expert Laurence Steinberg, "It is not a question of whether or not teens will experience peer pressure, but rather what kind of pressure."

Peer pressure exists in many forms. Parents think it is very direct—in your face. In reality, peer pressure can be much more subtle. It might happen when teens model a certain way to act or [are] supportive of what someone says or does as opposed to a directive.

Here is how one teen described a social situation in which alcohol was involved: "It's there if you want it, but nobody gives you a hard time if you don't. Like, no one comes up and shoves a beer in your hand and says, 'Here, drink it!' Of course, if everybody else is drinking you may feel a little weird just sipping a soda." Peer pressure comes from within and [may depend on] how much pressure teens place on themselves.

Not all teens react to peer pressure in the same way. Gender and age are factors. For example, boys are more susceptible than girls to peer pressure, particularly in risk situations. Younger teens are more easily influenced than older teens, with peer pressure peaking in about eighth or ninth grade. In-

Peer Pressure Can Be a Positive Influence on Children

Peers provide encouragement and challenge to engage in positive activities. A good example is the popularity of Harry Potter books. Many parents are overjoyed to find their children reading what their peers are reading. Peers can provide positive pressure to join a soccer team, stop bad habits, work on community projects, eat healthier, or even set up a business. Peers also ease some of the stress in the major transitions in life by providing security and confidence. Peers listen, understand, and provide a sounding board. Children need to go out in the world and test the values learned at home. The peer group is the next logical step in the world, as well as peers' parents and other adults in the workplace, and volunteer settings.

Judy Arnall, "Can Peer Pressure Ever Be Positive?"
Calgary's Child Magazine, August 3, 2006.

dividual characteristics such as confidence level, personality and degree of maturity make a difference. Peer pressure varies according to the situation: being with one close friend, in the small clique of friends, or seeing what the larger peer group is doing in school.

Often, parents want to blame their teen's friends for negative behavior. Actually, they need to look at why their teen chose those friends in the first place. No doubt there were similar interests there. Friends do not redirect a teen's choices and behaviors, but reinforce what was there to begin with. If a teen already has strong feelings or beliefs about an issue and is comfortable with those views, he or she will most likely stick to them.

Parental Influence

Sometimes parents of teens feel as if they have no influence at all. In reality, it depends on the issue. Teens are influenced by peers on current pop culture choices such as music, fashion, activities and appearance. While these are very important to the teen at the time, they don't decide the future.

Teens are influenced by parents on longer term issues, including college and vocational choices, political, moral and religious concerns. That influence can lead to parents and teens having similar views, with variations based on peers and changing social opinion.

Understanding peer pressure better will help parents understand their teen.

Periodical Bibliography

The following articles have been selected to supplement the diverse views presented in this chapter.

Neil Bernstein   "Sex and Peer Pressure," MSNBC.com, January 26, 2005.

Carl Bialik   "Online Warnings Mean Well, But the Numbers Don't Add Up," *Wall Street Journal*, January 21, 2005.

Alan Cohen   "Do You Know Where Your Kids Are Clicking?" *PC Magazine*, June 21, 2006.

Naomi Dillon   "Schools Now Must Prepare for a New Threat: Armed Intruders," *School Board News*, October 24, 2006. www.nsba.org.

Economist (US)   "The Horror: Murder in School," October 7, 2006.

Brooke Gladstone   "Prime Number," NPR's *On the Media*, May 26, 2006. www.onthemedia.org.

Sunniej Jackson   "Keeping Our Children Safe from Internet Predators," BellaOnline, 2007. www.bellaonline.com.

National School   "School Security Should Be a Top Priority,"
Boards Association   *School Board News*, April 9, 2006. www.nsba.org.

Record Online   "When Students Fit the Profile," March 24, 2005. http://archive.recordonline.com.

Lynn Stuter   "Cause and Effect—The Virginia Tech Tragedy," NewsWithViews.com. April 24, 2007.

U.S. Immigration and   "Operation Predator," January 23, 2007.
Customs Enforcement

Pete Williams   "Despite Killings, Schools Are Safer, Experts Say," *NBC News*, March 22, 2005.

OPPOSING VIEWPOINTS® SERIES

CHAPTER 4

What Would Ensure the Safety and Health of Young Adults?

Chapter Preface

Social networking Web sites and the risks they pose to young adults have been a hot topic of late. Millions of minors hold accounts with MySpace, Facebook, and other sites where users display a profile with their personal information and connect with people around the world. Unfortunately, some nefarious adults use these sites to disguise their identities, lure youngsters into meeting them in person, and cause them harm. One 14-year-old girl, for example, was allegedly sexually assaulted by a 19-year-old man posing on Myspace as a high school senior. In response to such occurrences, the Deleting Online Predators Act (DOPA) was introduced in 2006 by Republican senator Michael Fitzpatrick. It called for schools and libraries to block youths' access to social networking sites or else lose certain federal funding. House Speaker Dennis Hastert expressed his support for the bill: "We've all heard stories of children on some of these social Web sites meeting up with dangerous predators. This legislation adds another layer of protection." The law, however, was met by bitter protest from those who charged that it would encroach on the civil liberties of minors and adults who use the sites legitimately. The battle over this ban is just one of many in the debate over what measures ought to be used to protect children.

The very nature of the Internet, where users can easily disguise their age, sex, and true intentions, seems to lend itself to predatory attacks. The Police Notebook sums up the essence of the problem: "Predators on the net thrive on the anonymity of the interface." Furthermore, children, it appears, have not been navigating the Internet safely. A survey by *Seventeen Magazine* estimates that 12 to 14 percent of teenaged girls have met strangers from the Internet in person, a statistic that alarms online safety experts and many parents. According to a Department of Justice memo, "Adult predators are very serious about their bad intentions, and they are relentless." When they have an encounter with youngsters, it "could very well prove to be a deadly one." Exacerbating matters, many youths are also pretending online to be someone they are not or to be older than they are. Therefore, supporters of DOPA claim, it is necessary to restrict use of social networking sites when young people are at school or the library where their parents cannot monitor their activities.

Critics, however, charge that the law is a form of censorship that would impede library users' access to useful information. Adam Thierer of Progress & Freedom Foundation laments that the government is attempting "to play the role of cyber traffic cop" and believes that it will "chill legitimate forms of speech or expression online." Opponents of the ban especially worry that it would extend far past the social networking sites it was meant to govern. Electronic Frontier Foundation contends:

> Protecting children online is important, but letting federal bureaucrats arbitrarily censor legitimate speech is the wrong way to go. . . . DOPA . . . potentially covers IM [Instant Messenger], blogs, wikis [collaborative Web sites], discussion forums, and other sites far beyond MySpace. Despite its limited exceptions, DOPA will restrict children's and adults' online research, distance learning, and use of community forums, among other activities.

Although the bill passed in the House in 2006, it stagnated in the Senate. The controversy continues into 2007 with the introduction of a new version, the Protecting Children in the 21st Century Act, by Alaskan senator Ted Stevens. Whether youths need more protective measures and which ones would best serve them is the central topic of the following chapter. The heated debate over Internet restrictions and other measures hints at the difficulty faced by legislators, teachers, parents, and youth advocates as they attempt to offer solutions that would protect children in the United States.

> "Longer stays in these treatment pro-
> grams can effectively decrease drug and
> alcohol use and criminal activity as
> well as improve school performance."

Inpatient Drug Programs Benefit Teens

Kimberly R. Martin

The National Institute on Drug Abuse (NIDA) researches the science behind drug addiction and publishes its results. In the viewpoint that follows, its NIDA Notes writer Kimberly R. Martin reveals that longer stays in community-based drug treatment programs benefit young people. A study NIDA commissioned examined over 1,100 adolescents, the majority of whom were in residential centers. The counseling, education, and support offered there helped curb adolescents' drug and alcohol use, criminal activity, and suicidal thoughts, the organization maintains. At the same time, the residents' self-esteem and school grades improved, in NIDA's view. According to one researcher in the viewpoint, these outcomes are impressive.

As you read, consider the following questions:

1. What elements of adult treatment programs does NIDA
   say were implemented in the youth programs?

Kimberly R. Martin, "Adolescent Treatment Programs Reduce Drug Abuse, Produce Other Improvements," *NIDA Notes*, vol. 17, April 2002.

2. According to the author, how did researchers verify adolescents' reports of their drug use?
3. What are considered to be the major drugs of abuse for young people, in NIDA's contention?

In the first large-scale study designed to evaluate drug abuse treatment outcomes among adolescents in age-specific treatment programs, NIDA-supported researchers have found that longer stays in these treatment programs can effectively decrease drug and alcohol use and criminal activity as well as improve school performance and psychological adjustment.

The study, part of NIDA's ongoing Drug Abuse Treatment Outcome Studies for Adolescents (DATOS-A), analyzed data from 23 community-based adolescent treatment programs that addressed peer relationships, educational concerns, and family issues such as parent-child relationships and parental substance abuse. Successful elements of adult treatment programs, such as participation in group therapy and participation in a 12-step program, were also included in treatment plans.

"The results of this study are particularly impressive in light of the fact that the adolescents had multiple problems," says Dr. Christine Grella of the University of California, Los Angeles (UCLA), Drug Abuse Research Center, one of the study's investigators. "Although this is also typical of many adults in treatment, timely resolution of these problems is even more critical for adolescents. These young people are in the process of developing values, making lifestyle decisions, and preparing to assume adult roles and responsibilities, such as family and work; whereas when many adults enter treatment, they have completed this process."

Three Treatment Programs

Dr. Yih-Ing Hser, also of UCLA, led the research team that evaluated the treatment outcomes for 1,167 adolescents, age

11 to 18, who were admitted to one of the treatment programs between 1993 and 1995. The treatment centers, located
in Pittsburgh, Pennsylvania; Minneapolis, Minnesota; Chicago,
Illinois; and Portland, Oregon, included eight residential programs, nine outpatient drug-free programs, and six short-
term inpatient programs.

The 418 adolescents in the residential treatment programs
received education, individual and group counseling, and interventions to develop social responsibility. The 292 adolescents in the outpatient drug-free programs received education,
skills training, and individual and group counseling. The 467
adolescents in short-term inpatient programs received counseling and a 12-step program. Family therapy was strongly
emphasized, and adolescents in these programs were referred
to continued outpatient treatment. The average length of treatment for adolescents in the residential, outpatient drug-free,
and short-term inpatient programs was 5 months, 1.6 months,
and 18 days, respectively.

The adolescents were interviewed when they began treatment and again 1 year after discharge by professional inter-
viewers who were not employed by the treatment centers.
Problem severity was determined at the initial interview according to a number of criteria. Dependence on drugs or alcohol was determined from standardized diagnostic measures.
To validate self-reports of drug use, one-quarter of the participants were selected randomly to submit urine samples during
the posttreatment interview.

Before treatment, 25 percent of the participants used three
or more drugs, 36 percent were dependent on alcohol, 64 percent were dependent on marijuana, and 10 percent were dependent on cocaine. In addition to substance abuse problems,
63 percent were diagnosed with a mental disorder and 67 percent were criminally active.

Behaviors of Adolescents Before and One Year After Treatment		
	Before	**After**
Drug Use	Percentage	
Weekly marijuana use	80.4%	43.8%
Heavy drinking	33.8	20.3
Hallucinogen use	31.0	26.8
Stimulant use	19.1	15.3
School Performance		
Regular attendance	62.6	74.0
Grades average or better	53.4	79.6
Criminal Activities		
Any illegal act	75.6	52.8
Any arrest	50.3	33.9

TAKEN FROM: Kimberly R. Martin, "Adolescent Treatment Programs Reduce Drug Abuse, Produce other Improvements, " *NIDA Notes*, April 2002.

Adolescents Enjoyed Positive Outcomes

Research has indicated that in general the rate of drug and alcohol use tends to increase during adolescence. In the present study, however, improvements were observed in many of the areas evaluated, although some of the participants did not complete their treatment program. Comparing the year before treatment to the year after treatment, the adolescents showed significant declines in the use of marijuana and alcohol, which are considered to be the major drugs of abuse for this age group. Weekly or more frequent marijuana use dropped from 80 percent to 44 percent, and abstinence from any use of other illicit drugs increased from 52 percent to 58 percent. Heavy drinking decreased from 34 percent to 20 percent, and criminal activity decreased from 76 percent to 53 percent. Adolescents also reported fewer thoughts of suicide, lower hostility, and higher self-esteem. In the year following treatment, more adolescents attended school and reported average or better-than-average grades. Some exceptions to the general pattern of improvement were that overall, cocaine and hallucinogen use did not improve during the year after treatment.

Previous research indicates that a minimum of 90 days of treatment for residential and outpatient drug-free programs and 21 days for short-term inpatient programs is predictive of positive outcomes for adults in treatment. Better treatment outcomes were reported among adolescents who met or exceeded these minimum lengths of treatment than for those who did not. Among the treatment participants, 58 percent of those in residential programs, 27 percent in outpatient drug-free programs, and 64 percent in short-term inpatient programs met or exceeded the minimum stay. In the year following treatment, those who met or exceeded the minimum treatment were 1.52 times more likely to abstain from drug and alcohol use and 1.2 times more likely to not be involved in criminal activity. In addition, these adolescents were 1.34 times more likely to have average or better-than-average grades.

This study confirms that community-based drug treatment programs designed for adolescents can reduce substance abuse and have a positive impact on many other aspects of their life, says Dr. Tom Hilton of NIDA's Division of Epidemiology, Services and Prevention Research. These results justify new research to identify the key elements common to effective treatment programs for adolescents, he noted.

> "Fear of cruel treatment kept me from
> seeking help [for drugs] long after I be-
> gan to suspect I needed it."

Inpatient Drug Programs Harm Teens

Maia Szalavitz

*Residential rehabilitation programs for drug-using teens are bru-
tally confrontational, overly restrictive, and even traumatizing,
alleges Maia Szalavitz in this viewpoint. Attempts to scare or
humiliate vulnerable youths into getting sober, she reasons, may
only exacerbate their problems. What's more, she claims, the programs are unregulated by federal law, leaving young drug addicts unprotected from emotional abuse, beatings, forced sleep
deprivation, and other methods that in extreme cases have resulted in death. Szalavitz authored the book* Help at Any Cost:
How the Troubled-Teen Industry Cons Parents and Hurts
Kids.

As you read, consider the following questions:

1. How many American teens are enrolled in public and
   private treatment facilities, in the author's estimation?

Maia Szalavitz, "The Trouble with Tough Love," *Washington Post*, January 29, 2006, p.
B01. Reproduced by permission of the author.

2. What are the two major problems with tough love treatment, as cited by Szalavitz?

3. What facts does the author present to support her notion that tough love tends to backfire?

My descent into drug addiction started in high school and now, as an adult, I have a much better understanding of my parents' anguish and of what I was going through. And, after devoting several years to researching treatment programs, I'm also aware of the traps that many parents fall into when they finally seek help for their kids.

Many anguished parents put their faith in strict residential rehab programs. At first glance, these programs, which are commonly based on a philosophy of "tough love," seem to offer a safe respite from the streets—promising reform through confrontational therapy in an isolated environment where kids cannot escape the need to change their behavior. At the same time, during the '90s, it became increasingly common for courts to sentence young delinquents to military-style boot camps as an alternative to incarceration.

But lack of government oversight and regulation makes it impossible for parents to thoroughly investigate services provided by such "behavior modification centers," "wilderness programs" and "emotional growth boarding schools." Moreover, the very notion of making kids who are already suffering go through more suffering is psychologically backwards. And there is little data to support these institutions' claims of success.

Little Regulation

Nonetheless, a billion-dollar industry now promotes such tough-love treatment. There are several hundred public and private facilities—both in the United States and outside the country—but serving almost exclusively American citizens. Although no one officially keeps track, my research suggests that some 10,000 to 20,000 teenagers are enrolled each year. A patchwork of lax and ineffective state regulations—no federal rules apply—is all that protects these young people from institutions that are regulated like ordinary boarding schools but that sometimes use more severe methods of restraint and isolation than psychiatric centers. There are no special qualifications required of the people who oversee such facilities. Nor is any diagnosis required before enrollment. If a parent thinks a child needs help and can pay the $3,000- to $5,000-a-month fees, any teenager can be held in a private program, with infrequent contact with the outside world, until he or she turns 18.

Over the past three years, I have interviewed more than 100 adolescents and parents with personal experience in both public and private programs and have read hundreds of media accounts, thousands of Internet postings and stacks of legal documents. I have also spoken with numerous psychiatrists, psychologists, sociologists and juvenile justice experts. Of course there is a range of approaches at different institutions, but most of the people I spoke with agree that the industry is dominated by the idea that harsh rules and even brutal confrontation are necessary to help troubled teenagers. University of California at Berkeley sociologist Elliott Currie, who did an ethnographic study of teen residential addiction treatment for the National Institute on Drug Abuse, told me that he could not think of a program that wasn't influenced by this philosophy.

Unfortunately, tough treatments usually draw public scrutiny only when practitioners go too far, prompting speculation about when "tough is too tough." Dozens of deaths—such as this month's [January 2006] case of 14-year-old Martin Lee Anderson, who died hours after entering a juvenile boot camp that was under contract with Florida's juvenile justice system—and cases of abuse have been documented since tough-love treatment was popularized in the '70s and '80s by programs such as Synanon and Straight, Inc. Parents and teenagers involved with both state-run and private institutions have told me of beatings, sleep deprivation, use of stress positions, emotional abuse and public humiliation, such as making them [residents] dress as prostitutes or in drag and addressing them in coarse language. I've heard about the most extreme examples, of course, but the lack of regulation and oversight means that such abuses are always a risk.

Why Does Love Have to Be Tough?

The more important question—whether tough love is the right approach itself—is almost never broached. Advocates of these programs call the excesses tragic but isolated cases; they offer anecdotes of miraculous transformations to balance the horror stories; and they argue that tough love only *seems* brutal—saying that surgery seems violent, too, without an understanding of its vital purpose.

What advocates don't take from their medical analogy, however, is the principle of "first, do no harm" and the associated requirement of scientific proof of safety and efficacy. Research conducted by the National Institutes of Health and the Department of Justice tells a very different story from the testimonials—one that has been obscured by myths about why addicts take drugs and why troubled teenagers act out.

As a former addict, who began using cocaine and heroin in late adolescence, I have never understood the logic of tough love. I took drugs compulsively because I hated myself, because I felt as if no one—not even my family—would love me if they really knew me. Drugs allowed me to blot out that depressive self-focus and socialize as though I thought I was okay.

How could being "confronted" about my bad behavior help me with that? Why would being humiliated, once I'd given up the only thing that allowed me to feel safe emotion-

The Peril of Group "Get Tough" Programs

The evidence indicates that "scare tactics" don't work and there is some evidence that they may make the problem worse rather than simply not working. One of the hazards of the juvenile court system is the impact of having a record on the child's subsequent life course. Such evidence as there is indicates that group detention centers, boot camps, and other "get tough" programs can provide an opportunity for delinquent youth to amplify negative effects on each other.

National Institutes of Health,
State-of-the-Science Conference Statement,
October 13–15, 2004.

ally, make me better? My problem wasn't that I needed to be cut down to size; it was that I felt I didn't measure up.

In fact, fear of cruel treatment kept me from seeking help long after I began to suspect I needed it. My addiction probably could have been shortened if I'd thought I could have found care that didn't conform to what I knew was (and sadly, still is) the dominant confrontational approach.

Fortunately, the short-term residential treatment I underwent was relatively light on confrontation, but I still had to deal with a counselor who tried to humiliate me by disparaging my looks when I expressed insecurity about myself.

Tough Love for Traumatized Kids

The trouble with tough love is twofold. First, the underlying philosophy—that pain produces growth—lends itself to abuse of power. Second, and more important, toughness doesn't begin to address the real problem. Troubled teenagers aren't usually "spoiled brats" who "just need to be taught respect." Like me, they most often go wrong because they hurt, not because

169

they don't want to do the right thing. That became all the more evident to me when I took a look at who goes to these schools.

A surprisingly large number are sent away in the midst of a parental divorce; others are enrolled for depression or other serious mental illnesses. Many have lengthy histories of trauma and abuse. The last thing such kids need is another experience of powerlessness, humiliation and pain.

Sadly, tough love often looks as if it works: For one thing, longitudinal studies find that most kids, even amongst the most troubled, eventually grow out of bad behavior, so the magic of time can be mistaken for the magic of treatment. Second, the experience of being emotionally terrorized can produce compliance that looks like real change, at least initially.

The bigger picture suggests that tough love tends to backfire. My recent interviews confirm the findings of more formal studies. The Justice Department has released reports comparing boot camps with traditional correctional facilities for juvenile offenders, concluding in 2001 that neither facility "is more effective in reducing recidivism [repeat negative behavior]." In late 2004, the National Institutes of Health released a "state of the science" consensus statement, concluding that "get tough" treatments "do not work and there is some evidence that they may make the problem worse." Indeed, some young people leave these programs with post-traumatic stress disorder and exacerbations of their original problems.

Based on Purely Anecdotal Evidence

These strict institutional settings work at cross-purposes with the developmental stages adolescents go through. According to psychiatrists, teenagers need to gain responsibility, begin to test romantic relationships and learn to think critically. But in tough programs, teenagers' choices of activities are overwhelmingly made for them: They are not allowed to date (in many, even eye contact with the opposite sex is punished), and they are punished if they dissent from a program's therapeutic prescriptions. All this despite evidence that a totally controlled environment delays maturation.

Why is tough love still so prevalent? The acceptance of anecdote as evidence is one reason, as are the hurried decisions of desperate parents who can no longer find a way of communicating with their wayward kids. But most significant is the lack of the equivalent of a Food and Drug Administration for behavioral health care—with the result that most people are unaware that these programs have never been proved safe or effective. It's part of what a recent Institute of Medicine report labeled a "quality chasm" between the behavioral treatments known to work and those that are actually available. So parents rely on hearsay—and the word of so-called experts.

> "Providing [emergency contraception] to adolescent women will decrease unintended pregnancies, reducing the number of abortions and teen parents."

Emergency Contraceptives Should Be Made More Available to Girls

Healthy Teen Network

To help young people make responsible decisions about sex, pregnancy, and parenting, the national membership organization Healthy Teen Network offers resources to professionals working in adolescent reproductive health. Healthy Teen Network insists in the following viewpoint that emergency contraceptive pills (ECP) are a safe, effective way for young girls to prevent pregnancy after having unprotected sex. Making ECP available to them without a prescription, the organization maintains, would decrease rates of abortion and teen parenthood as well as the risks associated with unintended pregnancy. The group denies that adolescents with access to ECP would become more promiscuous or more exposed to STDs.

Healthy Teen Network, *Emergency Contraception for Adolescents*, Washington, DC: 2005. Copyright © 2005 by Healthy Teen Network. Reproduced by permission.

As you read, consider the following questions:

1. What are four concerns with ECP, as outlined by Healthy Teen Network?
2. In the author's view, how many abortions were prevented in 2000 due to emergency contraception?
3. Name five risks faced by mothers who did not plan to get pregnant, according to the author.

The decision to allow over-the-counter (OTC) access to emergency contraceptive pills (ECP) for women 18 and older is an exciting development in reproductive health. Access to ECP for all women of reproductive age—including those under 18—is the logical next step in teen pregnancy prevention and achieving lowered abortion rates. Although approved for prescription only by the Food and Drug Administration (FDA) in 1999, knowledge of and about ECP by adolescent health care providers and pharmacists, as well as by adolescents themselves is often inaccurate or lacking; thereby limiting patient access to and use of ECP. In fact, only about 6% of women of all ages have ever used emergency contraception. Adolescents, unaware of a "back up" form of contraception, do not know they have secondary options to prevent unintended pregnancies. Besides overall awareness, there are other major ECP concerns: 1) Not all emergency rooms treating victims of sexual assault dispense ECP, or even inform patients of it and refer them elsewhere to receive it; 2) Recently [as of 2005], some pharmacists are claiming "moral authority" by refusing to fill prescriptions for ECP, and may also be declining to refer a patient to a pharmacist who will fill a prescription; 3) The FDA dual label ruling hinders access for adolescents 17 and younger by placing a time consuming and stigmatizing barrier between the teen and treatment.

FDA Approval

Plan B® was approved by the FDA in 1999, for availability by prescription in the United States. When approving Plan B® for

America's Youth

Emergency Contraception
Does Not Promote Teen Sex

Adolescents have been included in many of the studies showing that EC [emergency contraception] does not promote sexual risk-taking, and some research has focused specifically on adolescent and young adult women. A recent analysis of teen data . . . revealed that the teens did not take more sexual risks than women aged 20 to 24. The teens with increased access to EC also were no more likely to report being pressured to have sex. Teens are at greatest risk of unintended pregnancy because they are unlikely to see a family planning provider before or immediately after the onset of sexual activity and are more likely to rely on condoms as their primary method of contraception. Therefore, they have a great need for increased access to EC.

Tina Raine and Deborah Weiss,
"Does Emergency Contraception Promote Teen Sex?"
Contemporary OB/Gyn, *September 1, 2005.*

prescription sale, the FDA did not impose any age restrictions for users of the drug. Plan B® manufacturer Barr Laboratories submitted an application to the FDA, in early 2003, to switch Plan B® from prescription to over-the-counter (OTC) status. In 2004, although overwhelmingly approved by scientific advisory experts—and without age limitations—the FDA rejected the application. Barr Laboratories submitted further information for reconsideration, including a revised application for OTC availability for women 16 and older. Although the FDA commissioner Lester Crawford said a decision would be made by September 1, 2005, the FDA once again delayed a decision, arguing they were uncertain as to procedure on offering [a drugs as] an OTC drug to one age group, and [as a] prescription to another age group.

174

That same month, President [George W.] Bush nominated Dr. Andrew von Eschenbach as acting commissioner. On March 2006, Senator Patty Murray (D-WA) and Senator Hilary Clinton (D-NY) vowed to block Eschenbach's confirmation in protest to the FDA's OTC Plan B delays. One day before Eschenbach's confirmation hearing the FDA announced plans to meet with Barr and resolve issues regarding OTC Plan B® approval. Next day, Eschenbach affirmed his support of OTC Plan B® for women 18 and older during his confirmation hearing. On August 18, 2006, the FDA announced that Barr has resubmitted a Plan B® OTC application. Finally, on August 24, 2006, the FDA approved the OTC status of Plan B® for consumers 18 years and older, and maintained the prescription only status for those 17 and younger. This age restricted ruling comes without medical or scientific reasons or research to support it.

The Usefulness
of Emergency Contraceptives

In the United States, half of all pregnancies are unintended and over one-third of women become pregnant at least once before they reach the age of 20. The rate of unintended pregnancy in adolescents increases to 80%, with about one third of the 820,000 teenage pregnancies a year ending in abortion. In 2000, use of ECP prevented more than 50,000 abortions [in the] US. . . .

In 2004, births to 15 to 17 year olds fell to 133,980—the lowest it has been since 1950. CDC results indicated that a more effective and consistent level of contraceptive use was rising. They concluded that a recent upsurge of knowledge about general contraceptives and their increased use among adolescents significantly contributed to the decreased rate of teen pregnancy. This finding underscores HTN's [Healthy Teen Network's] core belief that all youth can make responsible decisions about their sexuality and reproductive health when they have complete, accurate and culturally relevant information, skills, resources and support.

Still, no contraceptive is foolproof. Over the counter ECP availability may have benefited the 22.1 out of every 1000 teenage girls between the ages of 15 to 17 years old who gave birth in 2004. In 2005, almost half of all high school students report having had sexual intercourse at least once. Access to ECP for all women of reproductive age is the next logical step in teen pregnancy prevention and achieving lowered abortion rates.

Impact on Behavior

Critics of ECP have expressed concern that adolescents' access to and use of ECP will increase sexual promiscuity and risky sexual behavior, as well as increase rates of sexually transmitted infections (STIs). However, research has shown that advance provisioning of ECP and ease of access to ECP does not affect adolescents' sexual behavior, nor increase their risk of STIs.

Conversely, unintended pregnancy can significantly affect the lifelong health and behavior of women, their children, as well as entire communities. Mothers of unintended pregnancy are at an increased risk of showing signs of depression, physical abuse, and not achieving their educational, financial and career goals. There is also an increased likelihood of interpersonal violence and three times a greater risk of relationship dissolution. Additionally, children of unintended pregnancies face an increased risk of low birth weight, dying in the first year of life, and higher abuse and neglect rates. Teen mothers are more likely not to finish high school and live in poverty.

In summary, providing ECP to adolescent women will decrease unintended pregnancies, reducing the number of abortions and teen parents. ECP are a safe and effective means to reduce unintended pregnancies and need to be accessible to women of all ages.

"STDs increased and abortions increased when Plan B [emergency contraception] was made easily available."

Emergency Contraceptives Should Not Be Dispensed to Girls

Janice Shaw Crouse

As director and senior fellow of Concerned Women for America's Beverly LaHaye Institute, Janice Shaw Crouse aims to bring biblical values into public policy. In the next viewpoint Crouse decries a plan to make emergency contraceptives available over the counter to young women. The drugs are dangerous, she contends, and they put teens at risk of contracting STDs. Equally worrying are the health effects of using emergency contraception routinely, which Crouse says teens are likely to do. The solution that would protect girls, she concludes, is to oppose legislation that would make such drugs easier to obtain.

As you read, consider the following questions:

1. What point does the author make about the prescription status of birth control pills versus that of Plan B?

Janice Shaw Crouse, "Plan B Over-the-Counter Is Beyond the Pale," Concerned Women for America, August 22, 2006. Reproduced by permission.

2. What is worrying about Plan B as it relates to STDs, in Crouse's opinion?

3. According to the author, what legal difficulties will be caused by Plan B?

As part of his strategy to be confirmed as the head of the U.S. Food and Drug Administration (FDA), nominee Dr. Andrew von Eschenbach threw his lot in with those who are lobbying to get Plan B, the so-called morning-after pill, available as an over-the-counter drug not requiring a doctor's prescription or supervision. Since late July 2006, Eschenbach and the FDA have been working with Barr Laboratories to pave the way for Plan B to be sold over-the-counter (OTC) instead of requiring a doctor's prescription (RX) before the drug can be dispensed. This week [in August 2006], that possibility came closer to reality when President [George W.] Bush announced his support for the Eschenbach plan—allowing OTC sales for 18-year-olds, but requiring an RX for teenage girls. [The plan was approved.]

A Pandora's Box of Problems

The major problem with the proposed compromise is that it is totally unworkable. It makes about as much sense as acting as though a car with air bags wouldn't need to have its brakes serviced and kept in good repair.

How can the FDA monitor a 2-track marketing strategy for the drug? How can the FDA enforce the age restriction? The regulatory issues and monitoring ramifications would be daunting. Worse, the plan would unleash a Pandora's Box of problems related to the conflicting roles of doctors and pharmacists in such a commercial arrangement.

In short, providing Plan B over-the-counter is beyond-the-pale.

Since birth control pills require a prescription and a doctor's supervision during use, how can the FDA or the drug

The Dangers of Increasing Teen Access to the Morning-After Pill

The federal Food and Drug Administration (FDA) will decide by the end of [August 2005] whether to allow over-the-counter (OTC) sales of the morning-after pill (MAP). The fact that it is even considering doing so is another example of the power of feminist dogma, a power that trumps threats to young women's health from this potentially dangerous and certainly unproven method of birth control and abortion. . . .

Feminists and their lackeys in the medical profession want the FDA to liberalize the availability of MAP. This will surely lead to the irresponsible repeated use of MAP, especially by teenage girls who fail to use conventional contraception.

Joseph A. D'Agostino,
"MAP's Medical and Abortion Problems"
PRI Weekly Briefing, *August 18, 2005.*

manufacturer condone providing Plan B (a mega-dose of the same drugs) over-the-counter? Widespread access to Plan B would expose women to the health risks that heretofore were acknowledged by doctors who screened women before prescribing birth control pills and then monitored them for the wide variety of contra-indicators for their use. Some of the health risks associated with birth control pills—life-threatening ectopic pregnancies, for instance—are a clear danger for some women with Plan B, too. Also, some physicians are concerned about the long-term effects of high-dosage birth control pills (Plan B) and others worry about their effect on adolescents and the fact that there are no constraints that would prevent repeated use of Plan B for "emergency contraception."

Leaving Girls Vulnerable

Having Plan B available over-the-counter is beyond-the-pale, too, because already those targeted for its use (under 25-year-olds) are experiencing an epidemic of sexually transmitted diseases. Plan B would offer no protection against STDs, of course, but would provide a false sense of security for those involved in risky sexual behavior and thus increase their risk of STDs. Several countries (Scotland and the United Kingdom, for instance) have discovered that STDs increased and abortions increased when Plan B was made easily available. In the United States, Planned Parenthood clinics that tracked their Plan B prescriptions also reported an increase in abortions.

Of equal concern is the fact that any 18-year-old could buy Plan B OTC and give it to anyone else—even underage girls—without parental consent or knowledge. The ramifications of such distribution include sexual abuse and sexual exploitation. The amount of misinformation about Plan B is astounding. Those advocating OTC availability are touting the drug as a "silver bullet" for birth control. Yet, the easy availability that would come with OTC sales extends to those who are incapable of understanding the risks involved in any high-potency drug. Highly vulnerable potential users would include young teens as well as those of limited intelligence or education who might not understand the dangers of using Plan B routinely.

The legal can-of-worms that Plan B unleashes is equally troubling. When something goes wrong, as it inevitably will, where will the victims turn? To the drug store? The pharmacist? Barr Laboratories? The FDA? Sadly, there will be no recourse for those who fall victim to this social experiment. America's women and girls are, once again, subjected to medical experimentation at the urging of those who want to be free of the consequences from sexually promiscuity regardless of the cost to their own or other women's health and well-being.

VIEWPOINT

> "Children whose parents monitor and
> control their access to violent media
> are less likely to demonstrate the nega-
> tive effects of such media."

Minors Should Be Required to Obtain Parental Consent to Buy Violent Video Games

Hillary Rodham Clinton, et al.

The viewpoint that follows is a bill introduced to the Senate in December 2005 by Democratic Senator Hillary Rodham Clinton. Her stated goal is to limit children's exposure to violent video games by prohibiting the sale or rental of such games to minors, she explains. This is necessary because, in Clinton's assertion, adolescents exposed to graphic video games and other media exhibit increased hostility and desensitization to violence even years later. Although this bill stalled in Congress in 2006, it is likely that a similar bill may be introduced in the future.

As you read, consider the following questions:

1. What did the 2000 Joint Statement to Congress say, according to Clinton?
2. How does Clinton define video games?

Hillary Rodham Clinton, et al., *Family Entertainment Protection Act*, S. 2126. December 16, 2005. www.senate.gov.

3. What penalty would store managers face for violating this law, as set forth by Clinton?

A bill to limit the exposure of children to violent video games.

This Act may be cited as the "Family Entertainment Protection Act."

Congress finds the following:

Research shows that exposure to video games, television, movies, and other forms of media has powerful effects on the development of children and adolescents and that such effects can be positive or negative depending on the nature and content of the media.

Past Research Shows a Connection Between Media Violence and Aggressive Behavior

Experimental research and longitudinal research conducted over the course of decades shows that exposure to higher levels of violence on television, in movies, and in other forms of media in adolescence causes people in the short-term and, after repeated exposure, even years later to exhibit higher levels of violent thoughts, anti-social and aggressive behavior, fear, anxiety, and hostility, and desensitization to the pain and suffering of others.

This evidence is so strong, it has been replicated in so many populations, and it draws on such diverse methodologies that a 2003 comprehensive review of the literature concluded "the scientific debate over whether media violence increases aggression and violence is essentially over" and 6 major medical and public health organizations, including the American Medical Association and the American Psychological Association, issued a Joint Statement to Congress in 2000 stating that research points "overwhelmingly to a causal connection between media violence and aggressive behavior."

Current Research Reveals that Video Games Are Influential

New research shows that exposure to violent video games causes similar effects as does exposure to violence in other media, including increased levels of aggression in both the short-term and long-term, and research shows that the uniquely interactive, engaging nature of video games may be especially powerful in shaping children's thoughts, feelings, and behaviors.

Research shows that children are more likely to imitate the actions of a character with whom they identify, and in violent video games the player is often provided with a behavioral script where he or she takes the point of view of the shooter or perpetrator.

Research shows that children are more likely to learn from behaviors that they repeat over and over again and behaviors that they are rewarded for taking, and in most video games, surveys show, players repeat actions over and over again, aggression goes unpunished, and perpetrators are rewarded for taking aggressive action

Self Regulation in the Video Game Industry

The video game industry, through the Entertainment Software Ratings Board, has created a system of self-regulation, and a system to provide information to parents about the nature and content of video games.

The Entertainment Software Ratings Board has determined that certain video games contain intense violence and explicit sexual content that makes them inappropriate for minors, and has rated these games Mature and Adults-Only.

Research shows that children whose parents monitor and control their access to violent media are less likely to demonstrate the negative effects of such media.

Parents rely on the Entertainment Software Ratings Board ratings system to protect their children from inappropriate material yet, numerous studies have demonstrated that young people can access Mature-rated games with relative ease.

There is a need to enact legislation to ensure that the ratings system is meaningful.

Definitions

In this Act, the following definitions shall apply:

(1) BUSINESS.—The term "business" means any ongoing lawful activity that is conducted—

(A) primarily for the purchase, sale, lease, or rental of personal or real property, or for the manufacture, processing, or marketing of products, commodities, or any other personal property; or

(B) primarily for the sale of services to the public.

(2) COMMISSION.—The term "Commission" means the Federal Trade Commission.

(3) ENTERTAINMENT SOFTWARE RATINGS BOARD.—The term "Entertainment Software Ratings Board" means the independent rating system, or any successor ratings system—

(A) established by the Interactive Digital Software Association; and

(B) developed to provide information to consumers regarding the content of video and computer games.

(4) VIDEO GAME.—The term "video game" means an electronic object or device that—

(A) stores recorded data or instructions;

(B) receives data or instructions generated by the person who uses it; and

(C) by processing such data or instructions, creates an interactive game capable of being played, viewed, or experienced on or through a computer, gaming system, console, or other technology.

Video Gamers Interview the Lawyer Who Campaigns Against Graphic Video Games

Video games are the most dangerous of all violent media, because they are interactive. You actually enter into doing the violence. Psychologists explain that interactive violence is a far more effective and quick means of behavior modification. But video games are a neutral technology. You can electrify or incinerate a city with nuclear fission. The fission is not the problem. The problem is what you do with it. Likewise, video games are tremendous teaching tools, because of their powerful nature, but what we do with them is what is problematic. . . .

In a free society, adults can pretty much get what they want and should. You gamers need to get off the "Jack Thompson wants to ban video games" nonsense. I had a kid in New York call me the other day screaming at me because of that. I said please, listen to my real position. He listened. He was a nice and polite guy. When I was done, he said "Hey, I agree with everything you have to say on this. This was very cool." I asked him what prompted him to call. He said, "Our eighth grade social studies class was talking about you, and I thought I would call you." I said. "Tell your teacher I will be happy to address the entire class by speaker phone so they can hear what my real views are as the industry's chief critic," and he said that was very cool.

Jack Thompson, interviewed by play.tm, January 4, 2007.

Prohibition on Sale of Violent Video Games to Minors

(a) IN GENERAL.—No business shall sell or rent, or permit the sale or rental of any video game with a Mature, Adults-Only, or Ratings Pending rating from the Entertainment

Software Ratings Board to any individual who has not attained the age of 17 years.

(b) AFFIRMATIVE DEFENSES.—

(1) IN GENERAL.—It shall be a defense to any prosecution for a violation of the prohibition under subsection (a) that a business—

(A) was shown an identification document, which the business reasonably believed to be valid, indicating that the individual purchasing or renting the video game had attained the age of 17 years or older; or

(B) had an established ratings enforcement policy—

(i) as evidenced by—

(I) cash register prompts reminding employees of that business to check for identification stating that a customer is of an appropriate age to purchase or rent a video game, or an established video game age identification training program for employees of that business;

(II) clear labels indicating the rating on each video game sold or rented by that business; and

(III) signs on the wall of the business property explaining, in simple, easy-to-understand language, the ratings enforcement policy of that business; or

(ii) as evidenced by an online age verification system, in the case of online sales.

(2) LIMITATION.—if a business is found to repeatedly violate the prohibition in subsection (a) despite the adoption by such business of an established ratings policy as described [earlier], such business shall be prohibited in any prosecution for a violation of this section from using any of the defenses listed in subsection (b).

(c) PENALTY.—The manager or agent of the manager acting in a managerial capacity of a business found to be in violation of the prohibition under subsection (a) shall be subject to a civil penalty, community service, or both not to exceed—

(1) $1,000 or 100 hours of community service for the first violation; and

(2) $5,000 or 500 hours of community service for each subsequent violation.

Annual Analysis to Prevent Ratings Slippage

(a) IN GENERAL.—The Commission shall contract with an organization with expertise in evaluating video game content and that has no financial or personal interest, connection, or tie with the video game industry, to determine, in a written report, on an annual basis, whether the ratings established by the Entertainment Software Ratings Board remain consistent and reliable over time.

(b) CONTENT OF ANALYSIS.—Each annual analysis report required under subsection (a) shall—

(1) evaluate a random sample of video games, representing the full menu of Entertainment Software Ratings Board ratings;

(2) determine whether each such rating has essentially the same meaning from year to year; and

(3) compare Entertainment Software Ratings Board ratings to independent, valid, and reliable rating systems ratings.

Secret Audits and Investigations

The Commission shall conduct, and make public the results of, an annual secret audit of businesses to determine how frequently minors who attempt to purchase video games with a Mature, Adults-Only, or Rating Pending rating are able to do so successfully.

(a) IN GENERAL.—The Commission shall conduct, to the extent practicable, an investigation into embedded content in video games that can be accessed through a key-stroke combination, pass-code, or other technological means to estimate—

(1) what proportion of video games contain embedded content that is inconsistent with the rating given to such games, and what proportion of the domestic market such games represent;

(2) what proportion of video games containing embedded content that is inconsistent with the rating given to such games are known to the video game manufacturer at the time of the commercial release of the game to contain embedded content, and what proportion of the domestic market such games represent; and

(3) whether video game manufacturers have the capacity to ensure that video games do not contain embedded content that is inconsistent with the ratings given to such games.

(b) SENSE OF CONGRESS.—It is the sense of Congress that whenever the Commission determines that the content of a video game, either immediately accessible or embedded but accessible through a keystroke combination, pass-code, or other technological means, is inconsistent with the rating given to such game, the Commission shall take appropriate action under its authority to regulate unfair or deceptive acts or practices in or affecting commerce as authorized under section 5 of the Federal Trade Commission Act.

(c) TIMING OF REPORT.—Not later than 1 year after the date of enactment of this Act, the Commission shall report to Congress the findings of its investigation under subsection (a).

Authority to Register Complaints

(a) IN GENERAL.—The Bureau of Consumer Protection of the Federal Trade Commission shall ensure that consumers can file complaints alleging that content-descriptions or labels on a video game are misleading or deceptive using the same Commission Consumer Complaint procedure by which the Bureau of Consumer Protection accepts complaints concerning other forms of unfair, deceptive, or fraudulent advertising, including through an easily accessible online filing system.

(b) REPORT TO CONGRESS.—The Bureau of Consumer Protection shall tabulate and report to Congress, on an annual basis, the number of complaints under subsection (a) levied against each video game manufacturer and business.

> "It is now well-established that modern
> videogames are entitled to full First
> Amendment protection."

Minors Should Not Be Required to Obtain Parental Consent for Violent Video Games

Lawrence G. Walters

Lawrence G. Walters is a media and Internet law attorney and chairperson of the Florida Bar's First Amendment Law Committee. In the following viewpoint he insists that allowing the unrestricted sale of violent video games is constitutional. Several court cases have examined the legitimacy of laws prohibiting such sales and, according to Walters, have overturned the laws based on lack of evidence that violent video games cause actual harm. He warns that legislators and family values groups will likely produce research that supposedly correlates video game playing with aggressive behavior in youths in order to justify a ban.

Lawrence G. Walters, "Sex, Lies and Videogames," *GameCensorship.com,* 2006. Reproduced by permission.

As you read, consider the following questions:

1. What taboo topics does Walters believe game developers will delve into since the creation of Second Life?

2. How does the author explain "strict scrutiny" in this viewpoint?

3. In which court case did the state allege that violent video games cause brain damage, according to Walters?

It has been said, "Censorship is the bastard child of technology." Technological advances in video gaming software have created a rapid evolution from 1970's arcade game technology to today's role playing games, featuring an almost life-like level of realism, which mirrors the natural world in all of its graphic violence and sexual activity. In tandem with electronic gaming's rapid evolution and realism has been a meteoric rise in popularity and revenues which now rivals that of the motion picture industry. This tremendous growth and change has also spurred protest from family values groups. The fact that violence, sex, and videogames seem to play well in the media has brought out a fair number of lawmakers, eager to prove their "family values" mettle by answering the call that something be done at the legislative level to control access by minors to this increasingly violent and sexually-explicit game content.

This article will explore the current efforts to control dissemination of graphic videogames at both the state and federal levels, and will discuss how such efforts have fared in the courts. This study will then give the reader an evaluation of the industry's future, and some suggestions as to how parental concerns can be balanced with the rights of game developers.

The Reality of Virtual Reality

Videogames have evolved from the primordial "*Pong*" to modern virtual reality in a relatively short time. As the little green aliens on the screen began to take on more lifelike characteristics, games started to deal with increasingly adult themes. Videogame developers were no longer hindered by the perception that "videogames are for kids," and they began to embrace the "darker" side of human activity. Today's games fascinate, terrify, repulse, and sexually arouse users with such intensity that some claim that it threatens the ability of users to separate fantasy from reality.

Online role playing games such as *Second Life*®™ allow users to create a virtual alter ego, and engage in the entirety of human activity, from land acquisition to dating—from sex to serial killing. It is only a matter of time before game developers will begin exploring deeply taboo subjects, such as pedophilia, incest, or rape. This potential has the videogame industry stepping back to ask itself whether any content boundaries exist, or if free expression rights should allow for examination of all these topics. At a recent sex and videogames conference, developers, attorneys, and sex therapists queried whether some degree of voluntary industry regulation would be appropriate in order to ward off government censorship. Opinions vary widely on this issue, and consensus appears to be elusive. The certainty is that videogames are destined to reflect elements of the human condition never contemplated by the developers of the innocuous Pong, and some backlash is likely to result.

Previous Legislative Attempts to Prohibit Sales to Minors

Already, six states have passed bills that restrict the sale of violent or sexually-explicit videogames. Similar bills are pending in several others. Fortunately for the videogame industry, the courts have thus far been uniformly protective of the game developers free expression rights, and have struck down these laws on First Amendment grounds. Importantly, the courts have unanimously held that videogames constitute protected "speech" under the Constitution, particularly given the extensive themes and artistic/literary content included in modern games.

State lawmakers have struggled to define what constitutes a "violent" videogame, and how such determinations should be made. Some have focused on specific acts of violence towards police officers, while others have attempted to use a modified "obscenity" test; focusing on whether the game has serious literary, artistic, political, or scientific value with respect to what is appropriate for minors. However, First Amendment jurisprudence dictates that the government may only regulate the sale and distribution of erotic, as opposed to violent, media. Only when an expressive work crosses a certain line of eroticism will the courts approve restrictions on otherwise protected speech. This counterintuitive dichotomy has served to frustrate many legislators, and their attempts to restrict the sale of violent videogames exclusively to adults have met with crushing defeats in the courts. It is unlikely, however, that this string of legal victories will continue unbroken. At some point, lawmakers will find the "sweet spot" of regulation, and pass a law that will be upheld.

The Difficulty of Demonstrating "Harm"

The first case to recognize the constitutional protections afforded to videogame content was *Interactive Digital Software Association v. St. Louis County*. The case was initiated as a challenge to St. Louis County's ordinance restricting the sale of violent videogames to minors. After denying the industry's motion for summary judgment, the District Court dismissed the complaint and upheld the Ordinance's constitutionality. The Eighth Circuit Court of Appeals reversed, on the grounds that the Ordinance violated the First Amendment. The Appellate Court focused on the fact that the county attempted to restrict access to violent videogames based specifically on their content, along with the alleged harms potentially befalling those who play them.

Where laws seek to regulate speech based on content, the courts are bound to analyze the laws under a very stringent method of legal review known as "strict scrutiny." Under this test, the government bears the heavy burden of demonstrating that the law is justified by a "compelling governmental interest," and that the least restrictive means have been used to achieve the interest. The strict scrutiny test has been the downfall of numerous videogame laws, given the inability of the state governments to demonstrate any actual "harm" resulting from violent videogame play, as would be necessary to satisfy the state's initial burden. In case after case, the state or local government seeking to justify the videogame restriction failed to come forth with any convincing evidence demonstrating that playing videogames causes any discernible harm to either children or adults.

In the next legal challenge, *Video Software Dealers Assn. v. Maleng*, the plaintiffs, including an industry trade association, challenged the State of Washington's ban on selling violent videogames to minors. The Washington statute prohibited only violence against a "public law enforcement officer." In attempting to justify the law, the State attempted to argue that the violent content regulated by the law fell into the category of "obscenity" and was "harmful to minors," under existing legal standards. However, the court rejected the invitation from the state to expand the definition of "obscenity" or "harmful materials" to include violence. In addition to faulting the government for failing to establish a sufficient governmental interest in regulating violence, the court invalidated the law based on the fact that it was unconstitutionally vague, in that it failed to precisely identify the range of videogames the State sought to regulate.

Violent Videogames Are Constitutionally Protected

Later challenge's met with a similar fate: The State of California passed *Cal. Civil Code* § 1746, restricting the sale of violent videogames, and requiring that the games carry a particular label identifying them as such. The content regulated under the Act involved any depictions of "killing, maiming, or assaulting of any image of a human being." The District Court threw out the law, holding that while the Statute was not unconstitutionally vague, it likely violated the First Amendment due to the government's failure to establish a compelling state interest in protecting minors from violent videogame content.

Illinois jumped into the fray, passing a statute prohibiting the sale of violent and sexually-oriented videogames to minors, requiring forced labeling, prohibiting self-checkout procedures, and requiring warning signs near points of sale. In ruling on the *Entertainment Software Association's* Motion for Preliminary Injunction against the law, the court noted that the State did not submit sufficient proof that violent videogames incited lawless action, aggressive behavior, or "brain damage" (as alleged by the State). The court ruled that the State's ability to regulate violence is limited to media inciting imminent lawless action. However, the State's mere desire to censor violent videogame content was insufficient to support a legitimate governmental interest, as required to support the legislation. A similar ruling resulted from the First Amendment challenge to Michigan's violent videogame legislation, which was enjoined in November 2005, on First Amendment grounds.

As a result of these legal (and other) challenges, it is now well-established that modern videogames are entitled to full First Amendment protection. This is significant since regulations impacting speech based on its content are presumed to be unconstitutional, and governed by a completely different set of legal rules and principles than legislation impacting just about any other topic. Consistently, state and local governments have faltered when attempting to establish a causal link between videogame violence and real world aggression—particularly in children. The anecdotal observations by sociolo-

The Parents' Job

If parents don't want their children playing violent video games, parents should raise their children to understand that violence is not morally acceptable, and parents should accept the responsibility of keeping their children away from these games, whether on the Internet, in public arcades, or places where young people congregate that might offer video games as a source of entertainment.

Lynn Stuter, "Banning Violent Video Games,"
NewsWithViews.com, June 3, 2003.

gists and psychologists in this regard have thus far been insufficient to justify a ban on the sale of expressive materials, even to children.

Bad News for Videogame Fans

The losses in court have not dissuaded censorship advocates from encouraging lawmakers to keep trying to pass these laws. For example, state lawmakers worked with one well-known anti-gaming figure to develop a Bill prohibiting the sale of violent videogames to minors in Louisiana, which cleared the state's legislature in June, 2006. However, a federal court quickly intervened and entered a Temporary Restraining Order barring its enforcement. Similar efforts continue in Florida, Utah, Maryland, Virginia, and Oklahoma. Nonetheless, any attempt to equate violence with explicit sexuality will likely be rejected by the courts, given the clear distinction recognized by established judicial precedent.

Undoubtedly, lawmakers will learn from their failed efforts in the courts, and attempt to tweak both their legislative and judicial strategies. One strategy may be to focus only on sexually-oriented videogame content. Efforts to restrict erotic videogames may receive a much warmer reception in the courts given the historical precedent referenced above. However, the continued viability of these arguments is not a sure thing. In 2004, the United States Supreme Court rendered its decision in *Lawrence v. Texas* wherein the Court invalidated the nation's anti-sodomy laws. The rationale used by the Court for its decision is important, and may lay the groundwork for a change in the approach to legislation based on enforcement of a "moral code." The majority of Justices in that case found that the government's interest in enforcing morality can no longer justify legislation affecting fundamental freedoms. In fact, this revolutionary decision caused Justice [Antonin] Scalia to lament the potential demise of all laws premised on morality, such as those prohibiting prostitution, bigamy, bestiality, and importantly: obscenity. Although one district court picked up on this concern, and struck down the federal obscenity statute based largely on *Lawrence v. Texas*, that decision was later reversed by the Third Circuit Court of Appeal. The full impact of the *Lawrence v. Texas* case is not yet known, however, the winds of constitutional change may be blowing in favor of erotic expression.

Some change could be in the works regarding how violent content is addressed by the courts as well, but that change may be detrimental to the videogame industry. As mentioned above, in striking down previous regulatory attempts to date, courts have largely relied upon the lack of evidence of "harm" allegedly caused by videogame violence. However, family values groups are focused on generating scientific evidence to justify restrictions on violent videogames, particularly with regard to consumption by minors. These groups realize that the courts will not "rubber stamp" legislative attempts to restrict access to videogames just because some county council or state legislature thinks it's a good idea. Moreover, the government will be unable to meet its censorship burden by simply calling some hack psychologist or scientist to the stand to testify as to anecdotal incidents of violent behavior by teens after playing certain videogames. The censors have learned that "real" evidence is required, if the courts are to begin taking their arguments seriously. The industry can therefore expect to see mounting evidence in the form of studies suggesting a link between real world violence, and exposure to violent videogames. The initial studies are starting to come out. To the extent that these studies are not discredited—either by challenging their conclusions or their methodology—the government may begin achieving more success in the courts, when seeking to justify violent videogame legislation.

> "Not only are parent-adolescent rela-
> tionships and interactions generally
> positive, but they also matter."

Adolescents Need More Parental Involvement

Kristin A. Moore, et al.

The following viewpoint is excerpted from a brief produced by Kristin A. Moore and her co-researchers for Child Trends, a non-profit social science research group committed to improving the lives of children and their families. The researchers argue that positive parent-adolescent relationships are important to a child's wellbeing. The better the relationship it is, the more likely the child will make good grades, avoid trouble at school, and have higher self-esteem, they maintain. Furthermore, they assert, parents have more influence over adolescent children than they think and should invest time and effort into improving their relationship.

As you read, consider the following questions:

1. What are the five results of positive parent-child relationships, as stated by the authors?

2. What did the 2004 Child Trends poll discover about parents' views of peer influence versus parental influence?

3. According to the authors, what specific actions can parents take to strengthen their relationship with their adolescents?

Few would deny that it is intrinsically valuable for parents and children to feel close to one another and enjoy being with one another. However, . . . descriptive analyses do not address the related question of whether positive relationships matter for children's life outcomes. There is evidence from numerous research studies, though, that positive parent-child relationships and interactions enhance the development of children and adolescents. This literature is well-known to researchers who specialize in the topic; we summarize the findings here to share them with a broader audience.

Overwhelmingly, and despite variation in the way the quality of the relationship has been measured; research shows that positive and warm parent-child relationships are associated with more positive child and youth outcomes. Conversely, relationships that are less positive and warm have been linked to less desirable child and youth outcomes. This pattern persists across diverse populations, regions, and even across countries. Here, we present findings from several high-quality U.S. studies on this topic.

Benefits of Strong Parent-Child Relationships

Children and teens who have positive relationships with their parents tend to have better academic outcomes. Child Trends' analyses of the NLSY97 [National Longitudinal Survey of Youth, 1997] have shown that adolescents with high-quality relationships with their parents are subsequently more likely to have good grades and less likely to have been suspended from school than their peers with less positive parent-adolescent relationships, even after taking into account other social and economic influences. Similarly, parental involvement and connection with older teens (14-to-18 years old) predicts higher grades and higher academic expectations.

Good relations between parents and adolescents lessen the likelihood that teens will exhibit problem behaviors. Such behaviors have been well-studied and are regularly found associated with the quality of the parent-youth relationship. A roundup of findings from studies in this area are presented below:

- A study of more than 12,000 teenagers found a link between positive parent-child relationships and fewer violent behaviors.

- Similarly, another study found that teens with positive relations with their mothers (and their fathers) are less likely to be delinquent. This association is mediated by greater parental awareness about the adolescent, more supportiveness, and stronger family routines.

- Several studies have found that positive relationships or connectedness between parents and adolescents are linked to avoidance or lower use of alcohol, tobacco, and drugs.

- A review found that adolescents who have high-quality relationships with their parent were less likely to initiate sex or be sexually active, while another study found, conversely, that poor-quality parent-teen relationships were associated with increased sexual activity for females.

- Finally, studies have found similar links between the quality of the parent-child relationship and problem behaviors for sub-groups, as well, e.g., Mormon teens and both non-Hispanic white and Hispanic teens.

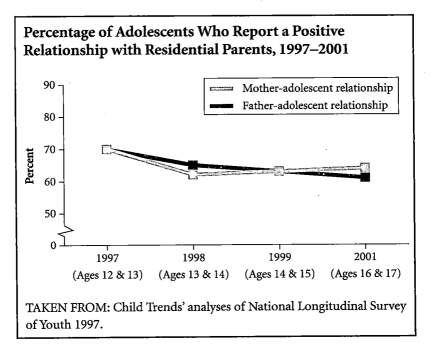

Percentage of Adolescents Who Report a Positive Relationship with Residential Parents, 1997–2001

TAKEN FROM: Child Trends' analyses of National Longitudinal Survey of Youth 1997.

High-quality parent-adolescent relationships have been linked repeatedly to mental, social, and emotional well-being in adolescents and youth. For example, analyses of the NLSY97 found that high-quality parent-adolescent relationships in early adolescence are linked to better mental well-being and less delinquency for the youth three years later, even after taking into account social and demographic characteristics of the family and the youth's prior behavior. Furthermore, across multiple multivariate longitudinal studies positive parent-adolescent relationships also are associated with self-confidence, empathy, a cooperative personality, and psychological well-being.

Lasting Results

Growing evidence indicates that the apparently strong influence of the parent-child relationship on child and adolescent outcomes extends into adulthood. For example, studies based on national survey data have revealed that, generally:

- Better quality adult child-parent relationships have been associated with lower levels of psychological distress among both adult children and parents;

- Close relationships with parents during childhood and adolescence have been positively associated with adult children's self-esteem, happiness, and life satisfaction; and

- Positive mental and physical health in adulthood is positively associated with recollections of early parental support.

Similar associations have been found in smaller-scale studies. These findings are encouraging, as research reveals that parents and their adult children are in frequent contact and report enjoying largely positive and rewarding relationships.

While many studies provide strong evidence of the link between positive parent-child relationships and child, teen, and even adult outcomes, it is also pertinent to acknowledge that there has been controversy about the importance of parents and that research certainly finds that peer influence also matters during adolescence. Indeed, a 2004 Child Trends public opinion poll found that only 28 percent of adults think that parents have a greater influence on teens than teens' friends or peer group. One-half of adults think that peers and parents have equal influence, while only one in four think that parents have a greater influence than peers. In addition, well-adjusted adolescents may interact with well-behaved, well-adjusted peers and *also* have quality relationships with their parents. However, the evidence that parents matter is very compelling. Clearly, it is not possible to conduct experimental studies to assess cause and effect, because one could not randomly assign children to parents. Still, nonexperimental research studies consistently find that parents are a critical influence in the lives of their children, adolescents included, even after controlling for the effect of the adolescent's prior behavior on the quality of the relationship with their parents. . . .

Thus, not only are parent-adolescent relationships and interactions generally positive, but they also *matter*.

Troubled Parent-Adolescent Relationships

At the same time, it is critical to acknowledge that some adolescents do not feel close to their parents. In the NLSY97, nearly four in 10 teens report that they do not have highly positive feelings about their parents. In fact, about one in 20 adolescents strongly disagree that they "think highly of" and "want to be like" their residential mother or father. . . . These attitudes are more likely when adolescents live apart from a parent and when their residential parent is not their biological parent. Even in these instances, though, a substantial proportion of adolescents hold quite positive feelings toward their parent or stepparent.

However, for that minority of teens who hold negative views, there is reason to be concerned. Supporting healthy marriages to help parents stay together or helping noncustodial parents remain involved in their children's lives may help some parents remain or become closer to their children. In other cases, parents may need to put time and effort into developing stronger relationships with their children, for example, by spending more time together and communicating regularly or by obtaining counseling. Becoming more aware that parent-adolescent relationships and interactions matter during the teen years may convince parents that this investment of time and effort is worthwhile, even if their teen appears uninterested at present.

Of course, parent-child closeness and parental involvement need to be age-appropriate. As children go through adolescence and become young adults, they do need to become more independent and responsible. For example, it would be inappropriate to monitor an 18-year-old as closely as a 13-year-old. However, research suggests that 18-year-olds continue to benefit from love, advice, values, and an ongoing sense that their parents care about what they do and what happens to them.

The Importance of Parental Influence

No one would argue that childrearing is an easy task, or that adolescence is a trouble-free period of development. Unfortunately, one-half of adults in the Child Trends poll think that peer influence is more important than parental influence. If parents mistakenly believe that their adolescent children don't care about them or respect them or enjoy spending time with them, a real risk exists that parents will step back from being involved in their children's lives. Since research consistently indicates that adolescents develop better when they feel close to their parents, it would be a serious loss to all concerned if parents acted as if they were no longer important once their children entered adolescence. Indeed, during the years of identity formation, as adolescents complete their education and develop vocational plans, and during the time when many teens face numerous risks that can undermine their future, it could be argued persuasively that positive parent-adolescent relationships and interaction are extremely important.

VIEWPOINT

> *"Just think of how many social problems could be reduced and even eliminated if Dads just stuck around—active, involved, caring."*

Adolescents Need More Father Involvement

Bill Stanczykiewicz

According to Bill Stanczykiewicz in the following viewpoint, children who live without their father suffer negative consequences. They are more likely to live in poverty, to use drugs, and to commit crimes than youths who live with two parents, according to national surveys. Such problems could be avoided, he suggests, if fathers remained active in their children's lives, whether it's by providing discipline, helping with schoolwork, or playing with their kids. Stanczykiewicz is president and CEO of the Indiana Youth Institute, which promotes the health development of children and youth by serving the institutions and people of Indiana who work on their behalf.

As you read, consider the following questions:

1. According to Child Trends, one-third of fathers are highly involved with their children in what areas?

Bill Stanczykiewicz, "Responsible Fatherhood Is No Field of Dreams," Indiana Youth Institute, June 3, 2004. Statistical information has been updated to be current as of June 2007. Reproduced by permission.

2. Which dads are celebrated on Father's Day, in Stanczykiewicz's opinion?

3. How does the author describe *Field of Dreams* as it relates to fathers?

"P*ING!*"

For veterans of the community baseball diamond, one of the memorable sounds of summer is the deep, textured *"CRACK"* of the wooden bat sending a baseball into play. But today's Little Leaguers, who know not the wooden bat, are accustomed only to the shallow, staccato *"PING"* of the ball hitting aluminum.

Despite this difference, baseball can still bridge the generations.

An Involved Father

The game already was underway when a Dad, running late from work, walked up to the side of the dugout to let his son know he had arrived. Moments earlier, the boy had laced a thrilling RBI single to right, giving his team the early lead.

"Hey, Dad. Did you see my hit?" the boy asked anxiously. "Yes, I did," his father replied. "I was walking toward the field from the parking lot, and I stopped to watch when I saw you were at the plate. Nice job taking the pitch to right field."

It was difficult to determine who was more excited. The dad, proud of his slugging son. Or the boy, affirmed by his father's encouragement.

As the dad took his place in the stands, he was greeted by another father and another question. "So how's everything at the office?" the friend said to the late-arriving fan. And they proceeded to talk shop while cheering on their boys of summer.

These two men on those well-worn bleachers continued making small talk by catching up on what was happening at

The Importance of Fathers

Father involvement makes a real difference. Whether the outcome is intellectual development, sex-role development, or psychological development, most kids do better when their relationship with Dad is close and warm, whether Dad lives with them or not.

Here are some findings about the unique role fathers can play in a child's life: . . .

- Children whose fathers were actively involved with them during the first eight weeks of life managed stress better as school-agers.

- Premature infants whose fathers spent more time playing with them had better mental outcomes at age 3, whether their father resided in the same house or not. . . .

- Children of highly involved fathers show increased cognitive competence, increased empathy, enhanced school performance, greater motivation to succeed, enhanced social development and self-esteem, less sex-stereotyped beliefs, stronger sexual identity and character, and more intrinsic motivation.

- Children of highly involved fathers have fewer psychological and behavioral problems, are less likely to become delinquent, and are less likely to use drugs.

Stephen F. Duncan,
Montguide, *June 2000.*

work. Not that this was a bad thing. After all, this conversation was occurring at the Little League field, where they watched and encouraged their kids. The Dads were there and into the game, and that's what matters.

Fatherless Children

More dads need to get into the game when it comes to parenting. According to the national research organization Child Trends, while two-thirds of dads play sports with their kids, only 33 percent are highly involved when it comes to other important activities like schoolwork, reading, puzzles, or board games. Just 40 percent limit the number of hours that their children watch television.

And that is when Dad is present in the home. In Indiana, 40 percent of all babies are born to single mothers, and 21 percent of Hoosier children and youth—more than 300,000 overall—live without their biological father. The consequences are costly.

According to the U.S. Census Bureau, 62 percent of children in single-mother households live in a family whose income is below $30,000 per year, and 39 percent of children living without Dad are living below the poverty level.

The financial fallout is just part of the story. According to national studies summarized by the National Fatherhood Initiative (NFI), "Children who live absent their biological fathers are, on average, at least two to three times more likely to be poor, to use drugs, to experience educational, health, emotional and behavioral problems, to be victims of abuse, and to engage in criminal behavior than their peers who live with married, biological (or adoptive) parents."

Just think of how many social problems could be reduced if more dads were involved with their children. This does not diminish the unique and vital role of Mom, and society certainly does not want kids connecting with violent or abusive dads who are a danger to themselves, let alone their children.

Children and youth need fathers who are caring, active, and involved. Dads who run and play, read and sing, hide and seek. Dads who take time to fix a bike instead of fax a document. And yes, dads who firmly set guidelines, provide discipline, and model strong character.

But for too many kids, including kids who now are adults, the final scene of the modern classic *Field of Dreams* remains too painful to watch. Ultimately, the movie is about redemption and second chances—for the scandalized former major leaguers who mystically and posthumously return to play on the enchanted field, and for the father and son who had split apart but never reconciled before the father's death.

The final dramatic question asked by lead character Ray Kinsella is bittersweet. "Hey, Dad. Do you wanna have a catch?" While Ray's father accepts the offer, the scene scrapes internal scars for viewers whose Dads were never there to be asked, and who were never there to say, "Yes."

We should not have to visit a field of dreams to experience responsible and involved fatherhood.

Periodical Bibliography

The following articles have been selected to supplement the diverse views presented in this chapter.

Danah Boyd and Henry Jenkins	"MySpace and Deleting Online Predators Act (DOPA)," *MIT Tech Talk*, May 26, 2006.
Hillary Rodham Clinton press release	"Senators Clinton, Lieberman Announce Federal Legislation to Protect Children from Inappropriate Video Games," November 29, 2005. www.senate.gov.
Wendy Cole and Thompson Falls	"How to Save a Troubled Kid?" *Time*, November 22, 2004.
Joseph A. D'Agostino	"MAP's Medical and Abortion Problems," *PRI (Population Research Institute) Weekly Briefing*, August 18, 2005.
David C. Dollahite and Alan J. Hawkins	"Fathering Teenagers," FatherWork. http://fatherwork.byu.edu.
Jason A. Martin	"Video Game Offensive: Family Entertainment Protection Act," December 19, 2005. www.jasonamartin.com.
National PTA	"When Kids Become Too Cool for Their Parents," Family Education Network. http://life.familyeducation.com.
Marc Polonsky	"The Myth of Tough Love," *Sun*, January 2007.
Tina R. Raine and Deborah Weiss	"Does Emergency Contraception Promote Teen Sex?" *Contemporary OB/GYN*, September 2005.
Marsha Rosenbaum	"A Reality-Based Approach to Teens and Drugs," NASP (National Association of School Psychologists) *Communiqué*, December 2004.
Maia Szalavitz	"Tough Love Quackery," presentation to Cato Foundation, April 20, 2006.
Jack Thompson, interviewed by play.tm	"Jack Thompson," January 4, 2007. http://play.tm.

For Further Discussion

Chapter 1

1. The author of the second viewpoint, Jonah Goldberg, adopts a mocking tone toward Democrats, young people, and others throughout his viewpoint. Do you find his method of argument effective? Is it more or less effective than that of his opposition, David C. King? Explain, citing the viewpoints in your answer.

2. While The Barna Group asserts that college-aged teens tend to lose their faith, Mark D. Regnerus and Jeremy E. Uecker counter that teens retain their faith but keep it more private during these years. With whom do you agree, and why? Develop your answer using points made in the viewpoints.

3. Re-read Peggy Kendall's viewpoint. How do you believe parents can best prepare their teens to face the challenges Kendall says are posed by technology? Support your answer.

Chapter 2

1. The viewpoints of Bradley Hope and Frank Greve were published around the same time and include evidence to bolster their assertions. Yet Hope concludes that juvenile crime is increasing while Greve insists that it is decreasing. What do you think might account for the contradictory evidence on which they base their claims?

2. In the third viewpoint, Laura Sessions Stepp posits that increasing occurrences of oral sex among teens may be correlated with abstinence-only sex education programs.

What do you think of her contention that teens substitute oral sex for intercourse as a result of their abstinence-only training? Support your answer.

3. The authors in this chapter focus on how the behaviors of youths have changed in recent years. Overall, do you feel teens are acting better or worse than in the recent past? Use examples from the viewpoints to develop your answer.

Chapter 3

1. Parry Aftab uses the case of murdered teenager Christina Long to make her point that online sex predators pose a major risk to youths. Benjamin Radford, by contrast, draws on several studies in his argument that young people are not likely to be approached by Internet predators. Which method makes for a more convincing argument, in your opinion? Why?

2. In the sixth viewpoint, Traditional Values Coalition analyzes claims that nearly one-third of teens who attempt suicide are gay. After reading the opposing viewpoint by Letitia L. Star, do you agree with the coalition's assertion that such statistics are exaggerated by gay activists in order to further their homosexual agenda? Why or why not?

3. Read the viewpoint by Margo Gardner and Laurence Steinberg as well as the one by Colleen Gengler. How big a role do you think peer pressure plays in the average teen's life? How big a role does it play in yours? Support your answer.

Chapter 4

1. In her viewpoint Maia Szalavitz admits to being a drug addict who stayed in a residential treatment center when she was young. Does this information validate her stance against inpatient rehab centers in your opinion? Why or why not?

2. Janice Shaw Crouse belongs to Concerned Women for America, an organization that aims to bring biblical values into public policy. The viewpoint before that organization was written by the Healthy Teen Network, an organization that supports adolescent health professionals in the fields of teen pregnancy prevention and teen parenting. How does this information help explain the authors' stances on whether teens should have access to emergency contraceptives?

3. Hillary Rodham Clinton contends that violent video games desensitize adolescents by teaching them that aggression is something to be rewarded. Do you find this argument convincing? Why or why not?

4. The authors in this chapter use varying types of evidence to support their notions. Choose two viewpoints and assess the evidence given by their authors, noting whether you think each type of evidence is credible, necessary, and used effectively.

Organizations to Contact

The editors have compiled the following list of organizations concerned with the issues debated in this book. The descriptions are derived from materials provided by the organizations. All have publications or information available for interested readers. The list was compiled on the date of publication of the present volume; names, addresses, phone and fax numbers, and e-mail and Internet addresses may change. Be aware that many organizations take several weeks or longer to respond to inquiries, so allow as much time as possible.

ABA Juvenile Justice Center
740 Fifteenth St. NW, Seventh Floor, Washington, DC   20005
(202) 662-1506 • fax: (202) 662-1507
e-mail: juvjus@abanet.org
Web site: www.abanet.org/child/juvenile-justice.shtml

Part of the American Bar Association, the Juvenile Justice Center disseminates information on juvenile justice systems and laws that pertain to youths. The center provides leadership to state and local practitioners, judges, youth workers, and policy makers. It supports school violence prevention and speaks out against the death penalty for minors. Among its publications is the quarterly *Children's Legal Rights Journal.*

American Civil Liberties Union (ACLU)
125 Broad St., Eighteenth Floor, New York, NY   10004-2400
(212) 549-2500
e-mail: aclu@aclu.org
Web site: www.aclu.org

Through litigation, education, and advocacy, the ACLU works to defend Americans' civil rights guaranteed by the U.S. Constitution. Seeking to protect the rights of everyone, the ACLU has fought to oppose abortion restrictions for minors, most forms of censorship in schools, policies that discriminate against gay teens, and other measures that may abridge personal freedoms. The ACLU offers policy statements, pamphlets, the *Student Organizing Manual*, and the semiannual newsletter *Civil Liberties Alert*.

American Library Association (ALA)
50 E. Huron St., Chicago, Illinois 60611
(800) 545-2433
e-mail: library@ala.org
Web site: www.ala.org

As the oldest and largest library association in the world, the ALA aims to ensure high quality library and information services are accessible to all of the public. Because it works to promote intellectual freedom and the open flow of information, the ALA opposes mandatory Internet filters and book censorship in schools. Its Web site contains a section on censorship in school, information about ALA's Banned Books Week, articles, reports, and books published by the ALA.

Cato Institute
1000 Massachusetts Ave. NW, Washington, DC 20001-5403
(202) 842-0200 • fax: (202) 842-3490
Web site: www.cato.org

The Cato Institute, a libertarian public policy research foundation, is dedicated to limiting the role of government and protecting individual liberties. Some of the many topics it discusses are affirmative action in college admissions, Internet censorship, and abuse and inefficiency in America's schools. The institute produces the quarterly magazine *Regulation*; the bimonthly *Cato Policy Report*; the *Cato Journal* three times a year; a monthly audio CD; and numerous books, policy papers, and articles such as "Doing It for the Children" about childhood obesity.

Center for the Prevention of School Violence (CPSV)
1801 Mail Service Center, Raleigh, NC 27699-1801
(800) 299-6054

e-mail: megan.q.howell@ncmail.net
Web site: www.cpsv.org

As part of the North Carolina Department of Juvenile Justice
and Delinquency Prevention, the CPSV is a primary point of
contact for information, programs, and research about school
violence. As a clearinghouse, it provides information about all
aspects of the problem of school violence as well as possible
strategies for promoting safer schools and fostering the positive development of youths. One of its reports is *School Resource Officers: What We Know, What We Think We Know,
What We Need to Know.*

Family Research Council (FRC)
801 G St. NW, Washington, DC   20001
(202) 393-2100 • fax: (202) 393-2134
Web site: www.frc.org

Through promotion of Judeo-Christian values, the council
seeks to protect the interests of the traditional family, the institution of marriage, and parental autonomy and responsibility. FRC supports abstinence education, the teaching of intelli-
gent design in schools, and school prayer. It opposes televised
indecency and what it calls homosexual advocacy in schools.
On its Web site it makes available its fact papers, commentary,
and reports.

Media Awareness Network (MNet)
1500 Merivale Rd., Third Floor, Ottawa, Ontario   K2E 6Z5
   Canada
(613) 224-7721 • fax: (613) 224-1958
e-mail: info@media-awareness.ca
Web site: www.media-awareness.ca/english

MNet offers resources for parents, teachers, and others interested in media and information literacy for youths. It provides
links to the latest commentary, research, news, and statistics
on topics such as marketing aimed at children, the effects of
media violence and stereotyping on kids, and ways to protect

youths while they surf the Internet. One of its Teachable Moments activities is "Smoke Screen: Tobacco in the Movies," which encourages students to examine the portrayal of cigarettes and smokers on the big screen.

Office of Juvenile Justice
and Delinquency Prevention (OJJDP)
U.S. Department of Justice, 810 Seventh St. NW
Washington, DC   20531
(202) 307-5911 • fax (202) 307-2093
e-mail: Askjj@ncjrs.org
Web site: http://ojjdp.ncjrs.org

OJJDP provides national leadership and resources to prevent and respond to juvenile delinquency. It supports community efforts to develop effective programs and improve the juvenile justice system. Publications available at its Web site include *Juvenile Offenders and Victims: 2006 National Report* and the Portable Guide *Use of Computers in the Sexual Exploitation of Children.*

Safeguarding the Wired Schoolhouse
Consortium for School Networking
1710 Rhode Island Ave NW, Suite 900
Washington, DC   20036-3007
(866) 267-8747 • fax: (202) 861-0888
e-mail: info@cosn.org
Web site: www.safewiredschools.org

Created by the Consortium for School Networking, Safeguarding the Wired Schoolhouse is a project designed to help school officials address the issues involved with Internet use and safety in schools. One of its resources is a toolkit designed to help school officials educate parents on the need to work together to promote Internet safety. It also offers a checklist for school decision makers, a PowerPoint presentation called "School District Options for Providing Access to Appropriate Internet Content," and links to various articles, reports, and Web sites.

Society for Adolescent Medicine (SAM)
1916 Copper Oaks Circle, Blue Springs, MO   64015
(816) 224-8010 • fax: (816) 224-8009
e-mail: sam@adolescenthealth.org
Web site: www.adolescenthealth.org

SAM is a multidisciplinary organization of professionals committed to improving the physical and psychosocial health and wellbeing of adolescents. It helps plan and coordinate national and international professional education programs on adolescent health. Its publications include the monthly *Journal of Adolescent Health* and the quarterly *SAM Newsletter*.

Teen-Aid, Inc.
723 E. Jackson, Spokane, WA   99207
(509) 482-2868
e-mail: teenaid@teen-aid.org
Web site: www.teen-aid.org

Teen-Aid is an international organization that promotes traditional family values and sexual abstinence until marriage. It publishes articles such as "HIV: You Can Live Without It" and a school curriculum called "Maturing in Body and Character" that encourages character development and abstinence.

Bibliography of Books

John C. Beck and Mitchell Wade *The Kids Are Alright: How the Gamer Generation Is Changing the Workplace.* Boston: Harvard Business School Press, 2006.

Rami Benbenishty and Ron Avi Astor *School Violence in Context: Culture, Neighborhood, Family, School, and Gender.* New York: Oxford University Press, 2005.

Sara Bennett and Nancy Kalish *The Case Against Homework: How Homework Is Hurting Our Children and What We Can Do About It.* New York: Crown, 2006.

Linda W. Braun *Teens, Technology, and Literacy; Or, Why Bad Grammar Isn't Always Bad.* Westport, CT: Libraries Unlimited, 2006.

Jane Delano Brown et al. (eds.) *Sexual Teens, Sexual Media: Investigating Media's Influence on Adolescent Sexuality.* Mahwah, NJ: Lawrence Erlbaum Associates, 2002.

Jimmy Carter *Our Endangered Values: America's Moral Crisis.* New York: Simon & Schuster, 2005.

Randal D. Day and Michael E. Lamb (eds.) *Conceptualizing and Measuring Father Involvement.* Mahwah, NJ: Lawrence Erlbaum Associates, 2003.

Al Desetta   *The Courage to Be Yourself: True Sto-ries by Teens About Cliques, Conflicts, and Overcoming Peer Pressure.* Min-neapolis, MN: Free Spirit, 2005.

Michael Dorn   *Innocent Targets: When Terrorism*
and Chris Dorn   *Comes to School.* Macon, GA: Safe Havens International, 2005.

Joy Dryfoos   *Full-Service Schools: A Revolution in Health and Social Services for Chil-dren, Youth, and Families.* San Fran-cisco: Jossey-Bass, 2004.

Laura Finley and   *Piss Off!: How Drug Testing and*
Peter Finley   *Other Privacy Violations Are Alienat-ing America's Youth.* Monroe, ME: Common Courage Press, 2004.

Anastasia   *Totally Wired: What Teens and Tweens*
Goodstein   *Are Really Doing Online.* New York: St. Martin's Griffin, 2007.

Mike Haley   *101 Frequently Asked Questions About Homosexuality.* Eugene, OR: Harvest House Publishers, 2001.

Bernard E.   *Language of the Gun: Youth, Crime,*
Harcourt   *and Public Policy.* Chicago: University Of Chicago Press, 2006.

Raymond M.   *A Baby Doesn't Make the Man: Alter-*
Jamiolkowski   *native Sources of Power and Manhood for Young Men.* New York: Rosen, 2001.

Steven Johnson   *Everything Bad Is Good for You.* New York: Riverhead Trade, 2006.

Gerard Jones and Lynn Ponton *Killing Monsters: Why Children Need Fantasy, Super Heroes, and Make-Believe Violence.* New York: Basic Books, 2003.

Steven J. Kirsh *Children, Adolescents, and Media Violence: A Critical Look at the Research.* Thousand Oaks, CA: Sage Publications, 2006.

Michael E. Lamb (ed.) *The Role of the Father in Child Development.* 4th ed. New York: Wiley, 2003.

Judith Levine *Harmful to Minors: The Perils of Protecting Children from Sex.* Minneapolis: University of Minnesota Press, 2002.

Roy Lotz *Youth Crime in America: A Modern Synthesis.* Upper Saddle River, NJ: Pearson/Prentice Hall, 2005.

Hal Marcovitz *Teens & Volunteerism: Gallup Youth Survey.* Broomall, PA: Mason Crest, 2005.

Stephanie H. Meyer et al. (eds.) *Teen Ink: What Matters.* Deerfield Beach, FL: Health Communications, 2003.

Peter M. Monti et al. (eds.) *Adolescents, Alcohol, and Substance Abuse: Reaching Teens Through Brief Interventions.* New York: Guilford Press, 2004.

John T. Pardeck *Children's Rights: Policy and Practice.* New York: Haworth Press, 2006.

Benjamin Radford *Media Mythmakers: How Journalists, Activists, and Advertisers Mislead Us.* Amherst, NY: Prometheus Books, 2003.

Jamin B. Raskin *Youth Justice in America.* Washington, DC: CQ Press, 2005

Mark D. Regnerus *Forbidden Fruit: Sex and Religion in the Lives of American Teenagers.* New York: Oxford University Press, 2007.

Alexandra Robbins *The Overachievers: The Secret Lives of Driven Kids.* New York: Hyperion, 2006.

Anna C. Salter *Predators: Pedophiles, Rapists, and Other Sex Offenders: Who They Are, How They Operate, and How We Can Protect Ourselves and Our Children.* New York: Basic Books, 2004.

James T. Sears (ed.) *Gay, Lesbian, and Transgender Issues in Education: Programs, Policies, and Practice.* New York: Harrington Park Press, 2005.

David Williamson Shaffer *How Computer Games Help Children Learn.* New York: Palgrave Macmillan, 2006.

Christian Smith and Melinda Lundquist Denton *Soul Searching: The Religious and Spiritual Lives of American Teenagers.* New York: Oxford University Press, 2005.

Timothy Smith — *The Seven Cries of Today's Teens: Hearing Their Hearts; Making the Connection.* Nashville, TN: Thomas Nelson, 2003.

Laura Sessions Stepp — *Unhooked: How Young Women Pursue Sex, Delay Love, and Lose at Both.* New York: Riverhead Books, 2007.

Karen Sternheimer — *It's Not the Media: The Truth About Pop Culture's Influence on Children.* Boulder, CO: Westview Press, 2003.

James P. Steyer — *The Other Parent: The Inside Story of the Media's Effect on Our Children.* New York: Atria, 2003.

Maia Szalavitz — *Help at Any Cost: How the Troubled-Teen Industry Cons Parents and Hurts Kids.* New York: Riverhead Books, 2006.

May Taylor and Ethel Quayle — *Child Pornography: An Internet Crime.* New York: Brunner-Routledge, 2003.

Michael Thompson et al. — *Best Friends, Worst Enemies: Understanding the Social Lives of Children.* New York: Ballantine Books, 2002.

Jane Waldfogel — *What Children Need.* Cambridge, MA: Harvard University Press, 2006.

Index